Cape Crusaders

Real-life Stories About the Players, Coaches
and Volunteers, Who Make the Cape Cod
Baseball League the Premier Amateur Summer
Organization in America

By Mike Thomas

To Caleb
Happy 12th
Birthday

PUBLISH AMERICA

PublishAmerica
Baltimore

First printing

ISBN: 1-4137-6232-8 (softcover)
ISBN: 978-1-4489-7729-1 (hardcover)
PUBLISHED BY PUBLISHAMERICA, LLLP
www.publishamerica.com
Baltimore

Printed in the United States of America

To my wife, Michelle, and my daughter, Lily, who managed to put up with me while I spent night after night away from them, gathering information for this book. Also, to my four-legged buddy Lance, who stood by me each time I locked myself in the room to put this together. I miss you, pal.

Table of Contents

Introduction

"The one thing about the Cape league is that if you truly love the game of baseball, you cannot resist it. It is baseball the way it was meant to be played and the way I learned how to play it. To not fall in even deeper, almost unconditional, love with the game of baseball, once one has experienced the Cape league, is next to impossible."
–Sean Walsh, former GM of the Bourne Braves

The Cape Cod Baseball League's motto is: "Where the stars of tomorrow shine tonight," and no slogan could be more fitting for the nation's premier amateur summer baseball league.

When the top 200-plus young college players throughout the country come together to play on beautiful Cape Cod each summer, it is simply a baseball fan's dream. Where else can you get an up-close look at the country's best young talent, witness the struggles and successes they endure swinging the wooden bat for the first time, while taking in some of the most competitive, hard-nosed baseball on a gorgeous summer's night—all free of charge?

The players might not be as well known on the Cape as they will be in a few years when many of them will climb the professional ladder and reach their ultimate goal of playing ball in distinguished venues such as Fenway Park, Wrigley Field, and Yankee Stadium. Beyond the quality baseball it produces, the Cape Cod Baseball League offers fans, young and old, the unique opportunity to mingle with the players, share a laugh or two with them, collect an autograph, or simply shake hands with the best talent in the world of college baseball and the future major league heroes of many.

"After the players have their talk at the end of the game, we like to let all the kids go onto the field," said Bruce Murphy, GM of the Cotuit Kettleers. "A lot of the kids and players see each other at the clinics, and a lot of the players know the kids by name. We had one player from Harvard who knew every kid by name. He should've been a politician. But that's what's special about this league—the

7

closeness of the players to the community. It's very family orientated."

"I grew up in Chatham," said Matt Hyde, a former Cape Cod league bat boy, who eventually worked his way up to becoming an assistant coach in the CCBL, and is now the assistant baseball man at Harvard University. "When I was in elementary school, I could hear the guys hitting as the field is right there. I would find a way to sneak out of class. You had guys like Joey Belle, Scott Coolbaugh, Mark Sweeney, and Jeff Bagwell then, and I did pretty much whatever I could to go see those guys."

Hyde's passion for the sport is the norm for baseball fans on Cape Cod, who fully appreciate that the talent level right in their own backyard is second to none.

Andy Baylock, the long-time head baseball man at the University of Connecticut and former manager of the Cape league's Falmouth Commodores in 1973 and 1974, puts the numbers into perspective when looking at the abundance of talent in the Cape Cod league.

"There are about seven or eight (National Collegiate Athletic Association) sanctioned leagues in the USA," Baylock said. "You've got leagues like the Great Lake league, Shenandoah Valley, but there's no question the Cape Cod league is the best one. Forty-one miles is the longest trip, you've got a nice environment, housing situations.

"You have 35,000 kids playing college ball, 20 play for Team USA and that leaves 34,980 kids and 200 of them come to play in the Cape. The Cape Cod league is the kids' first choice."

For the people who live on the Cape and faithfully follow their summertime squads, baseball is a way of life. It's ten tiny towns vying for baseball's bragging rights. Each little town has its own following—from Wareham to Orleans. The will to win, from both the players' and the fans' standpoint, is greater than ever. Local baseball enthusiasts get to see their sport played at its finest. It's baseball in its purest form, where the best young college players from all parts of the country gather with one goal in mind—to take that next step in hopes of making a long-lasting career in the sport they so dearly love to play.

"I view the Cape league as a bridge between college and professional baseball," said John Wylde president/GM of the Wareham Gatemen, one of ten teams in the league. "Here, the kids are given the chance to play pro ball, and I say that with quotes around it. Here's a chance for them to go out there and make some mistakes and learn from them."

The egos are at an extreme minimum, perhaps because the players realize they are no longer the main man on their team or maybe it's because they're playing in front of numerous scouts on a daily basis. Whatever the case, it's a fan's delight.

"The one thing about the Cape league is that if you truly love the game of baseball, you cannot resist it," said Sean Walsh, former GM of the Bourne Braves. "It is baseball the way it was meant to be played and the way I learned how to play it. To not fall in even deeper, almost unconditional, love with the game of baseball, once one has experienced the Cape league, is next to impossible. If baseball is part of who you are, then the Cape league will only serve to augment that characteristic, almost making it borderline obsession."

Cotuit's Murphy caught Cape Cod baseball fever in 1988 and has been involved with the Kettleers ever since.

"I started in 1989," Murphy said. "In 1988, I went to a couple of games, went to a few more in 1989, met a few people, came to some meetings, and once you go to the meetings, you're hooked. Right away, I became vice president. I was in the right spot at the right time. I was then the president for two to three years and have been the GM ever since 1999."

For many of the players, this can truly be considered the beginning of their baseball life. If the definitive aspiration is to play professionally, there's no better place to initiate that dream and help make it a reality than on Cape Cod. During their three-month summer stay, these young men are taught a lot more than perfecting the art of the double steal or how to appropriately grip the screwball. Simply put, they discover how to grow up. They learn how to become big-league ballplayers and, more importantly, how to become big-league adults.

For many, it's their first time using a wooden bat for an entire season and that, combined with facing the nation's stiffest competition during a grueling five-game-a-week schedule, can lead to a level of frustration, which can ultimately result in failure. For these same players, it's also their first time experiencing life in a new part of the country. These eighteen-year-olds are given day jobs, set up by the league, to help pay rent to the families willing to take them in during their summer-long stay.

"Most of the guys who come here are a joy," said Hester Grue, president of the Brewster Whitecaps. "Most of them are still at that stage where they just love to play baseball. The Cape league is a very good test to see what these guys are made of, because most of them at this point have been the stars on their team and now they have to deal with ten teams full of stars. But how bad can it be for these guys? They're on Cape Cod, living with good people, and playing baseball."

Cory Snyder, who came to Harwich in 1983 from Brigham Young University and left as the Cape's all-time home run hitter with 22 in a season—a record which still stands—learned the adjustments he had to make on Cape Cod went well beyond the playing field.

"When Cory was here, he worked for me," said Steve Ring, who managed in Harwich for five seasons. "Cory made one run a day to the Barnside Tavern in Hanover. He drove a truck and delivered some produce. He was from the West Coast and the first thing he asked me when he got into the truck was 'what's the best way to get to the freeway?' I told him there were no freeways on the Cape. I told him you had roads and rotaries here on Cape Cod."

"I remember it being a long drive, and so I asked him where the freeway was," said Snyder, who was elected into the Cape Cod Baseball League Hall of Fame in November of 2003. "We still joke about that today."

Mike Amrhein, an infielder out of Notre Dame, who played for the Bourne Braves in 1996, was the typical college player coming to play ball on the Cape for the first time. There weren't many expectations en route to his journey to Massachusetts, but he left with one of the best experiences of his life.

"My goal was to be competitive and learn as much as I could," said Amrhein, who played two summers on the Cape after suffering an open dislocation on his finger diving for a ball in his first season. "There was a lot more than just the baseball part of it. My host family, the Dobbins family, was wonderful. They're one of the first things that come to mind when I think about my time there. It's families like them who make the Cape Cod league more special. I also remember the fog-outs, the bus trips, and that the food there was outstanding."

According to Amrhein, the competition wasn't bad either.

"It was an eye-opener playing against some of those guys," he said. "The first day, I faced Dan Reichert in a scrimmage game. He had a slider that just disappeared. It was not surprising he was a number one draft pick."

The Cape Cod Baseball League lists its inaugural game as having taken place in 1885 with a game between Sandwich and Barnstable. Since then, the league has undergone numerous facelifts, many of which are key to making the Cape Cod Baseball League what it has become.

"We used to have two leagues, Lower Cape and Upper Cape," said Arnold Mycock, the longtime general manager of the Cotuit Kettleers. "From 1950-59 the Cape was made up of local kids. Then a man by the name of Manny Pena, from the Sagamore team, started importing players and compiled a very good team. So in 1960, I wrote to the major leagues to see if they could help me by recommending some players. Only one guy, George Owen, a Phillies scout, returned my letters and made some recommendations. George was a former Harvard and Boston Bruin hockey player, and because of him, Cotuit adopted the Phillies logo. We just took the 'P' off it and put 'Cotuit' on it.

"The two leagues merged in the fall of 1962. The Lower Cape had four teams, Upper Cape had six. The interest in the local players was dying out, so in 1963 a new league was created."

"The league has gone through a number of phases," said Wylde. "Originally, it was town teams versus town teams and that truly meant that you had to be from that town. Then it got to having imports brought in where you could have three college players per team. Now, the players have to be in college and have college eligibility remaining."

The league's biggest move came in the 1960s, when it became sanctioned by the NCAA. The move was the first of many critical changes that would take place within the next twenty years, putting the league on the national map.

"In the sixties, the league was restructured," said Dick Bresciani, the Cape Cod league's former PR man and currently the vice president/public relations and archives of the Boston Red Sox. "The league decided to try and get some money from the major leagues, and in order to do that, it needed to be sanctioned. The NCAA was one of the biggest factors in getting the Cape league going mainly because it gave all the franchises a better opportunity."

According to Mycock, the league received a thousand dollar grant in 1965. Two years later, the grant increased to five thousand dollars and there was a bylaw change in the league stating no more than four players on a team could be non-college players. Also, no player could be older than twenty-four.

In 1970, an NCAA rule was put into place stating if any league received a grant of ten thousand dollars or more, it would strictly have to be made up of freshman, sophomores and juniors.

Wylde says the Cape Cod Baseball League then came into its own in the mid-80s, taking a giant step in front of the other amateur summer leagues.

"The Cape league really jumped from one of the top leagues to THE best in 1985 for a couple of reasons," Wylde said. "The first was a big move in 1985 when, under the leadership of (former commissioner) Fred Ebbett, the league adopted the wooden-bat rule.

"The second was pure luck and happened when the Alaska league had an internal falling out and split into two leagues."

In 1988, the Cape Cod league expanded from eight teams to the current ten, adding the Bourne and Brewster franchises. The Bourne squad elected to stick with the majority of teams, becoming the sixth franchise to be nicknamed after a major league team—the Braves—while Brewster was labeled the Whitecaps.

"Supposedly someone was out there looking at the bay and saw some white caps on the water," said Grue. "It doesn't mean we have white hats. I swear they came up with that name to torment me. Do you know how hard it is to find a wave logo?"

Actually, a contest was held in the town, asking locals to come up with the nickname for their new baseball team. According to the Whitecaps' inaugural team yearbook, 304 residents participated with William E. Turkington suggesting the name that eventually was chosen.

Probably the most impressive aspect of the Cape Cod league is how it is run by regular people who simply enjoy the game of baseball.

"What amazes me the most is that the league is run by volunteers," Grue said. "It's amazing you can field ten quality teams with all those volunteers. A lot of people spend their own money and spend a lot of hours dedicating their time, and it's just wonderful."

"It's hard to say how many volunteers we have because some teams have twenty, some have ten," said league president Judy Walden-Scarafile, "but I would say the league has somewhere between 150 and 200 volunteers.

"A lot of people have been involved for a long time. We have people come in and set up the concession stand, the announcers come in forty to forty-five minutes before the game, people come in to put up the banners. There's a lot of volunteer work that goes on and that's a very important part of the league."

The talented pool of players, of course, is what draws the fans to the games, and those players are rapidly becoming the major-league players of today.

In the 2003 Major League Baseball season, there were 190 players wearing big-league uniforms who had played in the Cape Cod league.

On certain days, the 2003 Boston Red Sox team, which dropped a seven-game series heartbreaker to the New York Yankees in the

American League Championship series, had its entire infield made up for former Cape Cod league players. Third baseman, Bill Mueller (Bourne '92); shortstop, Nomar Garciaparra (Orleans '93); second baseman, Todd Walker (Brewster '92); first baseman, Kevin Millar (Harwich '92); and catcher, Jason Varitek (Hyannis '91, '93) all donned CCBL uniforms.

The Houston Astros' "Killer B's"—Jeff Bagwell (Chatham '87,'88), Lance Berkman (Wareham '96) and Craig Biggio (Yarmouth-Dennis '82)—also experienced college baseball life in New England.

Walden-Scarafile expects the number of Cape Cod grads reaching the majors to increase in the very near future.

"We're going to break two hundred soon," she said. "We're at 190 now and we were at 183 the year before. I think what really shocks me is that the players are on such a fast track to the majors. Some of these guys leave the Cape and are in the big leagues in two or three years."

These days, the future stars of Major League Baseball are shining brighter than ever on Cape Cod.

Chapter 1
The Players

"The summer I played on the Cape is as vivid as any of the summers I spent in the majors."
—Mike Flanagan, Falmouth '72

"Probably the worst part about having a pro career was not being able to go back to the Cape in the summertime."
—Will Clark, Cotuit '83

The numbers are astounding. One out of every six ballplayers playing in the major leagues today has taken the baseball journey through Cape Cod, showcasing his talent in the nation's premier summer baseball league. Some arrived from well-known colleges with big-time credentials, while others developed their reputation here on baseball fields such as Guv Fuller Field, Clem Spillane Field, or Eldredge Park. The players view the Cape Cod league as a springboard to professional baseball and local fans view those same players as their own hometown heroes.

Lineup cards might be filled with unfamiliar names during the Cape Cod Baseball League season, but as time passes, many of those same names wind up stitched on the backs of big-league uniforms.

"Nobody had ever heard of Bobby Kielty before he came here," said Brewster Whitecaps president, Hester Grue of the Oakland Athletics outfielder, who was a home run shy of becoming the first modern-day Cape leaguer to win the Triple Crown in 1998 as a member of the Whitecaps. "Scouts didn't even know him. He wound up being the MVP that year. I really think if he didn't play in the Cape Cod league, he wouldn't be where he is today. To this day, his parents continue to send a check faithfully every year as a donation to us."

Kielty's story isn't all that uncommon.

Players like Jeff Reardon and Mike Bordick, who both had healthy, double-digit careers in the majors, also used the Cape Cod league as a spotlight in order to get some added attention. Jeff Trundy, the field manager for the Falmouth Commodores recalls Bordick's struggles for recognition.

"I also coached in Maine in the Portland Twilight league," said Trundy. "Mike Bordick played there and if someone told me then that he'd have this type of major-league career, I probably wouldn't have believed it.

"In his junior year, he went undrafted. He told me he had a chance to play in the Cape Cod league and I told him he had to go for it."

Most players come to Cape Cod on recommendations from their college coaches. Some of them are unfamiliar with the Cape Cod Baseball League and its rich tradition, while others simply can't get here quickly enough.

"Kelly Shoppach was the last cut for Team USA and we had talked to his coach at Baylor about him," said Harwich GM Mike DeAnzeris of the highly touted catching prospect with the Pawtucket (AAA) Red Sox. "He was cut on a Thursday. In the interim, Kelly called me and didn't get me. I called him back and his mother answered. I asked her to have Kelly call me and she told me he was driving to Cape Cod. He just jumped in his car and drove here from Texas. He played that Sunday and hit a home run. He certainly turned a lot of heads on the Cape."

Many past, present, and future big-league players point to the Cape Cod Baseball League as playing a vital role in getting them to the professional level. Each individual has his own unique Cape Cod story and many believe playing summer ball along the shorelines of Massachusetts was by far the best, and most significant, summer they've ever experienced.

KEVIN CASH

You could say Kevin Cash caught many by surprise.
Playing third base for the Falmouth Commodores in 1999, Cash

was the typical Cape Cod league baseball player. He came from a big-time college, was hoping to get drafted, and had heard from his older buddies who had played with him at Florida State how much fun they had playing on the Cape. He was from Tampa, so he had never spent any significant time away from the South. After his junior year as a Seminole, he made the trek to Massachusetts to show himself to another part of the country.

Little did he know that while he was away from home, his game would change. It was a change that would send him quickly through the minor leagues and bring him to big-league baseball.

First-year Falmouth coach, Jeff Trundy, gave Cash the opportunity to catch that season but admits it was more by default than an ingenious decision on his part.

"Two of our guys got hurt, and he came to us saying he'd like to give catching a shot," Trundy said. "We knew he might be thinking about catching next year at school but we never really thought about him catching up here. One of my assistants worked with him and he looked good back there. He was a natural."

Not bad for a guy who never owned a catcher's mitt prior to coming to the Cape.

The reality of catching at Florida State was nothing more than an extreme long shot because the Seminoles had a pair of quality backstops, and it was better for the team if he maintained his position at third base.

Cash never did catch a game in college, but when he came to the Cape Cod league, he caught the eyes of those who counted most—the scouts. In his first game behind the plate, his strong arm, quick feet and poise drew much attention.

"I got a chance to see Kevin play and he caught well when I saw him," said Mark Snipp, the Blue Jays' former assistant director of scouting. "He had soft hands, a good arm, and a quick release, and I thought he might hit OK, too. As a catcher, he was a prospect. As a third baseman, he's probably your average player. His defense stood out the most. He was an easy guy to throw to—he framed very well. He has a strong arm, and is very accurate with his throws. To me, it looked like he caught all his life—like he was born to do it."

"We were fortunate to be at the game he caught," said Chris Buckley, the Jays' former director of scouting and now a special assistant to GM J.P. Ricciardi. "He was mainly a contact hitter, so the fact that he caught made him a prospect."

Although his defense was his strength, Cash also carried a pretty good bat. That combination earned him the right to play in the 1999 Cape Cod League All-Star Game as an infielder. However, when it came time to warm up for the big game, Cash quickly grabbed a catcher's mitt for infield practice.

"Oh, I remember when he did that," said Cash's all-star coach Don Reed, who skippered the Wareham club that season. "Most guys don't want to get behind the plate and take that beating, but he did. I liked that about him. He had all the tools to be a catcher—quick feet, good arm, and he was a good athlete."

"He had gotten some interest as a catcher which enthused him," said Trundy. "A couple of teams were extremely interested in him and that solidified his interest in being a catcher. When he caught, he created interest. When he came to us and said he'd catch, we had no idea he'd be this good. I remember a lot of guys coming up to us to ask about him."

Three years later, Cash got the call to the major leagues and got his first at-bat at Fenway Park in September of 2002. In August of 2003, Cash was recalled by Toronto from Triple-A Syracuse and was traded to the Tampa Bay Devil Rays after the 2004 season.

"Kevin came up here undrafted as a junior and all of a sudden he changes positions and puts himself in a competitive situation in terms of scouts," said Trundy, who was named the Cape's top manager in 2004. "That just says what kind of athlete he is. It makes you wonder why this hadn't happened before. He's a take-charge type of kid and a quick learner.

"Let's face it, there was a little bit of luck there, too. If our catchers had stayed healthy, who knows what would've happened. The Cape league gave him an opportunity, but from his end, he made it possible, too. Playing in the Cape league, kids are given an opportunity, but not everyone takes advantage of it. Kevin Cash did."

TERRY STEINBACH

Plain and simple, Terry Steinbach loved to play baseball.

Fresh off a full college slate at the University of Minnesota, Steinbach made his first trip to the northeastern part of the country and landed in Cotuit in 1982, suiting up for a whole lot more baseball, playing basically a six-game-a-week schedule for the Kettleers.

"I just wondered why we weren't playing seven," Steinbach said. "Baseball is something I always wanted to do. I was playing all the time. It's just what I loved to do. I always thought if given the chance to play professionally, I would do OK. My goal was to just get a chance."

Steinbach significantly increased his odds of making it big by claiming the Cape Cod league batting title that season with a .431 average—the highest total in the last twenty-one years. He was also the league leader in hits (75) and RBIs (54), and capped the summer by earning the Most Valuable Player award. His 18 doubles, 129 total bases, along with his average, hits and RBI totals that season, remain team records.

Granted, his success came three years before the league turned to the wooden bats, but would that have made a significant difference in his numbers? Would he have hit .400 if he wasn't swinging an aluminum bat?

"Probably not. Maybe .399," he said, laughing.

George Greer, the Cape Cod League Hall of Fame coach who managed Steinbach in that 1982 season, coached many future big leaguers during his nine-year managerial stint on the Cape, but felt Steinbach was the best pure hitter he coached.

"He was probably the best hitter I had as far as producing base hits," said Greer, the former head baseball coach at Wake Forest University. "I was fortunate to have coached a lot of great players and he was one of them.

"I'd say the best all-around player I ever had was Ron Darling. The kid with the most potential was probably Will Clark. The guy with all the tools to be a successful player was Greg Vaughn."

John Schiffner, who has thirty years of Cape Cod league experience as a player, scout, coach, and manager, says he's never seen a hitter like Steinbach.

"It's tough to single out the top players I've seen in my time here, but the year Terry Steinbach had in 1982 was amazing," Schiffner said. "He just hit line drive after line drive. He had something like 72 (actually 75) hits in 44 games. You've got to be kidding me—72 hits?"

"Terry loved to hit so much, you'd have to be very careful with him," said longtime Cotuit GM, Arnold Mycock. "You'd have to watch him closely to make sure he didn't bat out of order. He was that anxious to get up to the plate."

"He really was a man among boys up there," said Bruce Crabbe, a Cape teammate and current hitting coach for the Oklahoma Redhawks—the Texas Rangers' Triple-A squad. "He was just an animal. He drove the ball and he was real aggressive up there."

Ironically, Steinbach, who spent fourteen years as a catcher in the major leagues, wasn't wearing shin guards and crouching down in front of the home plate umpire on the Cape. When playing defense, Steinbach, a college third baseman, spent his time patrolling the Cotuit corners.

"He came to us as a third baseman, and he played some third," Greer said, "but we had recruited a first baseman, who decided, for some reason or another, not to come. We also had Randy Asadoor at third base, so we decided to put Terry at first."

Steinbach was a ninth-round draft pick of the Oakland Athletics in 1983 and played third base during rookie ball in Medford, Oregon, and again in A-ball in Madison, Wisconsin.

It wasn't until 1985 when Steinbach was moved behind the plate, a change made because of Oakland's first-round draft pick in 1984.

"They drafted Mark McGwire and had him slated for third base," said Steinbach. "They came to me that year, asked me to catch, and sent me to the Instructional League. I wasn't chomping at the bit to catch, but I knew because of my physique, it might be beneficial to me. At that point, catching was a matter of survival for me."

After his first full season as a catcher, albeit a back-up role in Double-A in 1985, Steinbach became the Double-A starter the following year, was quickly promoted to Triple-A Huntsville and was eventually called up to the big leagues by the year's end.

"Dave Duncan, Rene Lachemann, and Jeff Newman were all tremendous teachers and they helped me make the adjustment to becoming a catcher," said Steinbach. "I didn't know if I could do it. I had foot quickness, not foot speed—I wasn't fast by any means—but I had foot quickness, which is important to a catcher."

He also had the offensive numbers, which, he thought, would also help make the transition a bit easier.

"I remember one game in my rookie year I had a couple of hits, and at the end of the game I got a tap on the shoulder and was told the manager wanted to see me," Steinbach recalled. "I'm thinking to myself 'wow, Tony LaRussa's going to tell me how well I hit.' We walk into the office, he shuts the door and now I'm really thinking this is going to be good. Then he comes out and says 'if you ever catch a game that poorly again, you're gone.' Before that, I thought the number one job for a catcher was offense, but boy was I wrong."

During his major-league career, Steinbach eventually found the right mix. He was able to carve his niche as a defensive backstop without letting his offensive numbers slide. Steinbach became a three-time American League all-star catcher and finished with 162 career homers and a .271 batting average.

Not only is he grateful to Duncan, Lachemann, and Newman for making his professional career a success, he can also thank Big Mac for pushing him away from third base.

"I've thanked him many times," he said. "In 1987, he and I were roommates. Back then, they'd pair up the rookies and we'd talk about that. We also talked about how he played in the Alaska League and how I played on the Cape."

Seventeen years ago, Steinbach was reminiscing about his days in the Cape Cod league with arguably the major league's most prolific home run hitter of all time, and today, much hasn't changed. His memories of the CCBL are still quite colorful.

"I absolutely loved my time on the Cape," he said. "Think about it, you're 19-20, getting semi-paid—I mean you're working a job, but you wouldn't have that job if you weren't playing ball. You have no debts, you're playing six days a week and you're getting recognized. How bad can that be?

"Playing on the Cape was great exposure. Some players knew scouts on a first-name basis, but I honestly didn't pay much attention to them. I couldn't even tell if they were scouts. If they had a radar gun, that might be a clue, but other than that, I didn't know if they were from Los Angeles, Philadelphia, or Oakland. I just figured I would let my numbers speak for themselves. I knew how I was playing. I knew if I had a good game or if I stunk that day."

Like McGwire, Steinbach also had the opportunity to play in Alaska, but had committed to the Cape first. An avid outdoorsman, Steinbach admits if he hadn't signed on the dotted line so early, he may have been the Alaska League batting champ.

"I love the outdoors," he said. "I love hunting, fishing. The Alaska league had called, and who knows, if I hadn't committed to the Cape, maybe I would've gone to Alaska.

"But it all worked out for me. It was my first time really seeing that part of the country and I absolutely loved it. I had a tremendous experience on the field, but I had just as much fun off the field. We had a great group of guys in Cotuit, and it was very common for four, five, six guys to get together after a game and go a beach or have a party at a host family's house."

On the field, Steinbach's job was hitting and playing solid defense. Off the field, his job was working for a law firm.

"I guess I was a semi-caretaker," he said. "I'd mow the lawn, take care of the pool, do some other yard maintenance, skim the pool, some remodeling, a ton of stuff. It was nice because it was pretty flexible, not a typical 9-5 job. If I got in late from a game, I could go in at 10."

Steinbach ended his major-league career six years ago with his hometown Minnesota Twins, a team he still associates with.

"I'm still semi-involved with Minnesota," Steinbach said. "My last year was 1999 and Jacque (Jones), Torii (Hunter) were rookies, Brad Radke, Joe Mays, and Eddie (Guardado) were all there, so there's still a connection with the guys. "Major League Baseball is like a fraternity. When you're young, you want to get in so bad, and once you're in, you won't ever get out."

Taking off the shin guards and catcher's mask for the final time was difficult for Steinbach, who admits he struggled knowing he would never play at the highest level again.

"It was tough for me to leave. The hardest thing was realizing you'll never compete at that level again. I still coach and I golf, but nothing has given me that adrenaline rush like I had while catching. I don't miss the eight months, 162 games and the emotional roller coaster of baseball—the winning and losing.

"Now, whenever I need an ego boost, I just head out to the park and have people tell me how good I was," he said with a laugh.

LANCE BERKMAN

According to his Cape Cod league coach, Lance Berkman was the exception to the rule.

"When a hitter starts off poorly playing in the Cape, it's very tough to have a good year," said Don Reed, who managed Berkman when the Houston Astros outfielder played for the Wareham Gatemen in 1996. "The frustration factor sets in and you start to doubt yourself as a hitter. What I used to do as a manager was if a guy was really struggling in the beginning of the season, I'd get him out of the lineup and sit him a game or two to make sure he didn't go in the tank early."

Getting used to playing every day, adjusting to the wooden bats and batting against the top collegiate pitchers in the country can be the recipe for hitting failure in the Cape Cod league.

"In the Cape, you might be facing a team's No. 5 pitcher, but he's actually someone's No. 1 or No. 2 in college," Reed said. "It can be a tough place for hitters."

Berkman, however, proved there was a small loophole in Reed's theory as he struggled mightily in the first week, but bounced back to capture the league's batting title.

Reed, the winningest coach in Cape Cod league history, pushed Berkman, along with a few other players, and the manager's work ethic, combined with an intense desire to improve his own baseball skills, rubbed off on Berkman.

"He used to get on Lance Berkman," said Joe Walsh, an assistant to Reed and now the Harvard University baseball coach. "He would go up to Lance and ask him what time he would be coming to the ballpark the following day. Lance would say, 'quarter of 4.' Don would say, 'see you at 1.' Lance also liked to shoot the breeze during batting practice and Don would get on him to work on things instead of talking.

"Lance was also kind of a chubby kid then and Don, who worked out a lot, would say, 'Lance, when are you going to come work out with me?' Sometimes they'd work out together."

According to Reed, Berkman's success had a lot more to do than simply refining his physical tools. Berkman was gifted with some pretty thick skin.

"Lance was one of the few guys to get off to a poor start and finish well," Reed said. "A lot of that had to do with his attitude. He was a very positive kid. His makeup was very good. He stayed the same whether he was 0-for-4 or 4-for-4. He handled failure very well and many kids up there don't handle failure well. He had a great mental outlook, and when he was 0-for-4, he'd just say, 'I'll get 'em tomorrow.' He kept the pressure off himself and that really helped him a whole lot."

As the '96 season progressed, there weren't many 0-for-4's in Berkman's box scores, and the only pressure he faced was from Wareham teammate Dan McKinley, an outfielder out of Arizona State.

"I remember that season, Dan McKinley absolutely caught fire with the bat," said Wareham president/GM John Wylde. "His batting average rocketed up the charts. I remember his parents would come up here, and it seemed like when they were here watching their son play, you couldn't get him out. In the meantime, Lance was working his butt off with Don Reed. Dan eventually cooled off a bit and Lance won the batting title."

"I'd get on him about the batting title," said Wareham teammate, Brad Winget, who roomed with Berkman that summer. "I'd go up to him and say, 'watch out. Dan's sneaking up on you.' He'd get pissed off. He really wanted that title."

Berkman, a power-hitting, two-time National League all-star out of Rice University, finished with a .352 batting average, but only hit one home run during that season—a shot off the foul pole.

"I've always hit home runs, but that one year I just hit one," he said. "I was really hitting the ball hard and it never bothered me that I wasn't hitting home runs."

Despite Berkman's success at the plate, he did manage to strike out against Harwich's Brian August, a third baseman out of Delaware, who pitched one inning of Cape Cod league ball in a mop-up role.

"Wareham was crushing us," said August. "I think it was 18-2 or something. We were using a bunch of pitchers and the coach (Mike Maack) asked me if I wanted to throw an inning. I remember I faced the top of the order, Kevin Nicholson (first-round pick of the Padres), Dan McKinley, and Lance Berkman. I struck out Berkman and got the other two to ground out."

"It's a neat deal playing there—the wood bats, the level of competition, and you get to experience playing every day," Berkman said. "They do a very good job of recruiting. The teams up there keep their finger on the college pulse. The pitchers all have good stuff and everyone in the Cape deserves to be there. It's definitely a big benefit to play up there."

"I'll tell you one thing I love about the league was watching these young guys work hard," Reed said.

"One thing that impressed me was that there were many, certainly not everyone, but there were always quite a few kids who would come early for some extra batting practice or come and work on their defensive skills. And I don't buy it that when these same guys make it to the big leagues and start making good money, they stop working hard. Either you work hard or you don't, and we always had guys working hard. Those are the guys who are playing in the big leagues or have played in the big leagues. Lance is definitely one of those guys."

BARRY ZITO

Barry Zito spent two summers playing for the Wareham Gatemen.

Some baseball people on the Cape may joke about the guys from the West Coast being a little bit different. Some others insist left-handed pitchers are a tad strange. Well, what happens when you combine the two?

You get Barry Zito.

Zito, the 2002 American League Cy Young Award winner with the Oakland Athletics, arrived on the Cape in 1997 and played two summers with the Wareham Gatemen. The crafty southpaw owned a nasty curve, a specific daily pitching regimen and a few off-the-wall maneuvers.

Jim Hubbard, the former GM of the Wareham Gatemen, happened to be out on the West Coast in the spring of 1997 to visit his son who worked for a company in California. While out there, Hubbard heard of a left-handed pitcher at Cal Santa Barbara, who had recently struck out thirteen straight batters. He decided to check him out for himself.

"Zito went to Cal Santa Barbara before going to USC," said Hubbard. "I wanted to see him while I was out there. He gave up a home run in the first inning of the game I saw and then he really settled down. His curve was outstanding.

"My wife and I went to dinner with Barry and his parents and he wanted to go to the Cape league. At the time, we had our roster filled, but I was trying like hell to get him. I at the very least wanted to get him on a team there. I don't remember the exact situation, but we were able to find a spot for him. He was a surfer and he wanted to know if he could bring his surfboard with him. I told him it would be best for him to leave the surfboard home because (Wareham coach) Don Reed would probably send him home if he brought it."

"There were so many funny little things about Barry Zito," said Wareham president/GM John Wylde. "He had a routine he literally had to follow down to the minute. He would long-toss at a certain time, but he had to long-toss with Brian Tallet. It had to be Brian Tallet. Then he'd move closer and throw with the catcher at a certain time, and then he'd throw in the bullpen and so forth.

"Right before his second summer with us, Barry's father Joe called me and asked me if I could get a 4-by-4 or 4-by-6 piece of wood for Barry. I'm thinking, 'what the heck does he want this for?' He used it as a balance beam. He would get on the beam and hold his front leg up and balance for about five minutes or so. People would drive by the house Barry was staying and see him in the driveway on a piece of wood with his leg up in the air.

"I remember one game when we were playing Bourne in the deciding game of the semifinals, and Barry was pitching an absolute gem. He had struck out something like ten or twelve players in five innings and we were ahead 6-0. I mean it was put it in the books.

Some kid hits a hard grounder back at Barry, who fielded it cleanly, but the ball got stuck in the webbing of his glove. Instead of tossing the glove to first base like I've seen some people do, he was frantically wrestling with the glove trying to get the ball out. The runner was safe and the ball broke the web. He had to borrow Phil Devey's glove. Wouldn't you know it, after that play Barry just blew up out there. He walked three, gave up a grand slam and we had to get him out of there. He was so focused out there, and when something went out of whack, he just lost it."

"Barry Zito was out there," laughed Harvard University baseball coach Joe Walsh who was Zito's pitching coach in 1997 and 1998 with the Gatemen. "He'd sit in the dugout with his orange ear plugs and pink sandals. He also had this huge watch. I mean it was bigger than some of the clocks I've seen.

"Barry was a very hard worker. He always had this routine he'd go through before a game—forty-five minutes of doing this, forty-two minutes of doing that. His sister also always used to come here and video tape him. I remember this one game when he's supposed to pitch, it's about three minutes before this game's about to begin, he's not ready. I'm doing whatever I can to delay the game.

"Well, he goes out there and pitches and gets absolutely rocked. After the game, I asked him what was wrong. He says to me, 'what's the state with the kangaroos?' I said, 'you mean Australia?' He said, 'yeah, the Outback. My sister's out there and they found a dead kangaroo. Only it wasn't really dead. It took off with my brother-in-law's jacket, and his keys were in the jacket.'

"He's looking at me with a straight face as he's telling me this. I had no clue what he was talking about. He was trying to tell me the reason he pitched poorly was because his sister was in the Outback trying to get a key off a dead kangaroo or something. You can't make this stuff up. I was left there scratching my head. To this day, I have no idea what he was talking about."

As wild as the story was, Zito managed to remain focused about his career—determined to reach the next baseball level.

"His confidence was extremely high," Walsh said. "Not only did he dream about making the big leagues, he always visualized himself with the pros. He'd ask me if I thought Randy Johnson would still be in the pros when he made it. He was so focused. If he didn't make it, I don't know what he'd do."

Although Walsh believed Zito, the West Coast's version of the Spaceman, had the stuff to reach the majors, he didn't think he'd have so much success so quickly.

"There were plenty of guys there throwing 95 or so and Barry wasn't one of them," he said. "He wasn't the most athletic guy—anyone could beat him in a race. He was not a physical specimen, but his confidence was high, he prepared very well, and he ate, drank, and slept baseball. He was just very, very focused."

Ben Sheets, Barry Zito
1998
Photo by Angela Johnson

Ben Sheets, left, and Barry Zito were teammates at Wareham.

In Wareham, Zito was the teammate of Ben Sheets, another future major-league hurler with the Milwaukee Brewers. Ironically, when it came playoff time, neither one was considered the ace of the Gatemen.

"Going into the playoffs, we had Ben Sheets, Barry Zito, and a guy by the name of Phil Devey," Walsh said. "We threw Devey number 1, threw Sheets number 2 and we thought Zito would be better at number 3.

"One thing about Ben Sheets was, in order to get him ready for a game, you'd have to get nose-to-nose with him, scream at him, and tell him to go out there and shove it up their butt. You'd have to pump him up a little. If you didn't do that, he'd go out and get hit."

Zito's antics even continued in the big leagues when a group from Wareham went to see him pitch at Fenway Park against the Red Sox.

"When Barry was in the Cape, he lived with Lou the Barber," said Walsh. "He had a very good relationship with Lou. Before the game, he spots Lou in the crowd and yells 'Lou, Lou' and then he dives into the stands. Fans are wondering what the hell's going on. Art Howe's yelling for him to get back onto the field.

"Barry's a great guy, a hard worker, and a lot of fun. But he's a little off the wall."

While Zito's antics can be considered a bit unique, the Oakland southpaw maintains a heart of gold.

"My wife plays the cello," Wylde said. "One winter, her teacher had come down with cancer and he is a huge baseball fan. My wife asked me if we could get someone like Barry Zito to give him a call. Barry called him and talked to him for about twenty minutes. At first, her teacher thought it was a friend playing a trick on him. But it wasn't. It was Barry being Barry. That's just the way he is. He's a true gentleman."

Barry Zito
1998
Photo by Jeff Tamagini

Barry Zito

MIKE FLANAGAN / BILL ALMON

Mike Flanagan, the eighteen-year veteran major-league pitcher who hurled fifteen seasons for the Baltimore Orioles, spent the summer of 1972 playing for Falmouth in the Cape Cod Baseball League. Not only was the crafty southpaw, who attended nearby University of Massachusetts, busy baffling opposing hitters, he gave their pitchers a headache as well.

"I was among the league's leaders in home runs," said Flanagan, the vice president of operations for the Orioles. "I got to play in the outfield on the days I didn't pitch, but I always felt the best avenue to the majors was through pitching."

"To me, there was no doubt he was going as a pitcher," said former Falmouth assistant coach, Andy Baylock, the long-time head baseball coach at the University of Connecticut. "He had a great arm and he was a left-hander.

"He was a tremendous athlete, a great talent. He could also hit the ball. I remember during batting practice, he'd be in the outfield and he was able to catch a fly ball in his back pocket."

Flanagan finished his season on the Cape with a 7-1 record and a 2.18 earned run average. He also chipped in with seven homers when he was at the plate.

Flanagan apparently chose the appropriate career path as he chalked up the American League Cy Young Award in 1979 (23-9, 3.09), the same year he guided the O's to the World Series.

Flanagan's Cape teammates included the 1974 No. 1 draft pick Bill Almon and Los Angeles Dodgers bench coach, Jim Riggleman. His manager was Bill Livesey, now a special assistant to the general manager for the New York Mets.

"Mike Flanagan was just a real good athlete," said Almon, who played his college ball at Brown University. "He was a great basketball player, too. He could hit the ball a ton. He hit some towering home runs. He had tremendous power and was just a real good athlete. We played against each other in college and crossed paths a few times in the major leagues.

"When he was drafted, I remember asking if he was going as a pitcher or an outfielder. When I heard he went as a pitcher, I wondered if they would ever use him as a DH."

Despite his major league success, Flanagan looks back at his time on Cape Cod with nothing but genuine satisfaction.

"I am a little biased toward the Cape," said Flanagan, a native New Englander who grew up in New Hampshire. "There's no question in my mind the Cape Cod league is the elite summer league. It's the last measuring stick before turning pro. The summer I played on the Cape is as vivid as any of the summers I spent in the majors.

"Orin Taylor, who was my Little League coach, had a summer house in Bourne, and he let me and John Olson, a college teammate of mine, let us have use of the house while playing in the Cape."

Livesey was inducted into the Cape Cod League's Hall of Fame in 2002 as a manager, and Flanagan was enshrined the previous year.

"Playing for Bill Livesey was a precursor to playing for Earl Weaver," said Flanagan.

Livesey also played a major role in luring Almon to play on Cape Cod.

Ironically, when Almon attended Brown University, Livesey was the head baseball coach there and it was Livesey's affiliation with the Cape that made Almon's decision to attend Brown a bit easier.

"(Livesey) told me he was one of the coaches in the Cape league and he could get me to play there," said Almon. "That was one thing that really interested me in Brown—the connection to the Cape.

"I committed to Brown early, sometime in November or December of my senior year. The combination of an Ivy education, the baseball program and the opportunity to play on the Cape was too good to pass up."

Like Flanagan, Almon's ties to the northeast make him a bit partial to the Cape Cod Baseball League.

"I'm prejudiced, but prestige-wise I'd say it's the best amateur summer league," he said. "The whole experience was great. Ninety-eight percent of the kids playing in the Cape league have the ambition to go on professionally and that, to me, made playing more interesting. I got a real good taste of what it was like to play at the next level."

Almon also had invitations to play in other summer leagues, including the Alaska league, but simply decided to stay in New England.

"I did have an opportunity to play in the Alaska league, but I couldn't see traveling four thousand or so miles to do something I could do right at home," he said.

DARIN ERSTAD

When it came to working hard, nobody did it better than Darin Erstad.

Erstad came to the Cape as a freshman out of Nebraska in 1993 and it didn't take him long to make an impression on his Falmouth coach.

"I remember when he came here in '93, he drove non-stop from North Dakota," said Ace Adams, who was the head coach of the Commodores in 1992 and 1993. "He pulls up in my driveway—how he found my house, I'll never know—and says, 'Are you Coach Adams? I'm Darin Erstad.' Then he asks me if I would mind throwing him some batting practice.

"I said, 'let's go.' We head to Falmouth, to the batting cages, and he hits for about an hour. All I keep thinking to myself is that I can't screw this kid up. Just don't screw this kid up. I knew right away this kid was going to be special. Once you've been coaching for a while, you can tell right away if the player's got something, and Darin Erstad certainly had something."

It was likely Erstad had the itch to get on the diamond because he never played high school baseball.

"They didn't have baseball where he went to high school," said Falmouth GM Chuck Sturtevant. "He was very good in track and he was a hockey star."

Erstad also could play some football, as he was the punter on the University of Nebraska's 1994 national championship football team.

"While he was here, he would practice field goals of 60 yards," Sturtevant said. "In the '94 season, he had to leave during the playoffs because Tom Osborne wanted him back at Nebraska by August 5. We didn't do very well without him."

"Darin and I drove to every game together," said teammate Jason Garman, a pitcher out of Princeton. "Sometimes we'd be at his host's house and he'd punt to me. I remember one time we were there, the phone rang and Darin asked me to get it. They asked for Darin Erstad and I asked who it was and it was Coach Osborne."

"He always had a football in his car," said Mike Martin, a Falmouth teammate of Erstad in 1993. "He was a great all-around athlete and just the all-American kid. Hands down, Darin Erstad was the hardest worker I've ever seen. When you come to play on the Cape, a lot of guys can get distracted with everything that goes on there, but Darin was so focused. He was never distracted. My mother loved him when he was here, and she still talks about him when she sees him on TV.

"When we were there, we'd switch school stuff," said Martin, who attended Boston College. "Darin and I switched batting practice shirts and to this day I still have his Nebraska jersey."

Martin and Erstad shared team MVP honors during that summer of '93 and were elected, along with two other Commodores, to play in the all-star game.

"Darin was such a class act," said Don Nestor, a teammate of Erstad's, who was one of those Falmouth all-stars. "He was an outstanding guy who never said a bad thing about anyone. I remember him being such a nice person. There is no way he can be as generous today as he was back then. I also remember him having a thing for the trainer. Nothing ever came of it, but he did have a thing for her."

While Erstad was a well-rounded person and a well-rounded athlete, baseball was clearly what he did best.

"He could really hit," Sturtevant said. "His two year combined batting average was .340. He's the first guy who played in the '90s to be inducted into the Hall of Fame."

"In the first game of the year, at Hyannis, Darin steps up to take batting practice," said Garman. "I'm sure he took seven or eight hacks, and he may have hit every one out. It was amazing. "My uncle (Tommy Herr) played pro ball for fourteen years," Garman said. "He came up to one of our games and he looked at Darin and later said to me, 'that kid's going to be a big-league player.'"

MICKEY MORANDINI / ROBIN VENTURA

In the 1987 Cape season, the batting title came down to the wire. Hyannis' Robin Ventura, a pure hitter who came out of Oklahoma State as a sophomore after hitting safely in fifty-eight straight games, was battling with the relatively unknown Yarmouth-Dennis infielder Mickey Morandini out of Indiana University.

"It came down to the last day," Morandini said. "Robin was big then—not that he's not big now—but he was a first-round pick and one of the best hitters in the country. I was just this little white boy from Indiana."

Morandini finished the season as the batting champion, compiling a .376 average despite never using a wooden bat for any length of time. He also led the league in stolen bases with 47. Not only did Morandini walk away with the hitting and base-running titles, he left Cape Cod as the 1987 Most Valuable Player.

"It was the first time I'd ever used wood in a full season," Morandini said. "I was a little worried it would take a while to get used to, but I felt very comfortable up there at the plate."

The wooden bat was also fairly foreign to Ventura.

"I hadn't used a wooden bat since maybe Little League," he said. "I think everyone probably had trouble adjusting the first week. You start to get used to it when you're around it all the time and then you learn to make the adjustments. The fun part of the league was using those wooden bats and playing against a lot of very good players."

A native of the West Coast, Ventura didn't know much about Cape Cod, but he did hear a little bit about baseball on the Cape.

"My assistant coach at school was a head coach up there and he told me about it," said Ventura. "I grew up in California, so I didn't know anything about the Cape. I heard the Cape Cod league was a good league and it was a fun league to play in."

For Morandini, the Cape Cod league provided a boost to his confidence after he realized he could play with the high-profiled college players in the country.

"It was big for me to be able to compete at that level. There were a lot of guys there from schools like Oklahoma State, Miami and Arizona—schools that play around one hundred games a year—and I went to Indiana, where I wasn't used to seeing so many scouts. It was a tremendous experience for me and it definitely helped me get ready for the next level."

According to his manager Don Reed, Morandini was able to handle the pressure of playing in the Cape Cod league. More specifically, didn't let the stress of competing with the high-profiled Ventura get to him.

"That was quite a battle between Mickey and Robin Ventura," Reed said. "But one of Mickey's strengths was not worrying about things he couldn't control. He was able to put everything out of his mind, and this is why I always believe he would make it big."

Like Morandini, Ventura wasn't concerned with his personal statistics.

"I wasn't worried about winning the batting title," Ventura said. "We were just trying to get to the playoffs. I remember Mickey had a good run."

Morandini went on to enjoy an eleven-year career Major League Baseball career and played in the 1993 World Series as a member of the Philadelphia Phillies.

"He was the type of guy that if he stayed healthy, you knew he'd play a long time," said Reed, who recruited Morandini to the Cape. "He could flat-out hit. He was a consistent hitter, an intelligent baserunner and he had very good hands as an infielder.

"When we recruited him, we had some very good reports on him. He had his priorities in order. He was everything we expected and a whole lot more. He was a good leader—not real vocal—just led by example. He came to play every day and gave you everything he had."

ERIC WEDGE

He may not have had a lengthy major league career as a player, but Eric Wedge is likely to last a whole lot longer managing in the big leagues.

Wedge came to the Cape in 1988 as a high-profiled catcher out of Wichita State and was the third-round draft pick of the Boston Red Sox in 1989. Wedge played in parts of four seasons in the majors before a rash of injuries forced him to hang up his playing shoes.

If not for those injuries, Wedge, the manager of the Cleveland Indians, would likely still be enjoying those playing days in the majors.

"I'll tell you what, if Wedgie didn't get hurt, he would've been a superstar," said Don Reed, Wedge's coach at Yarmouth-Dennis. "He was an absolute throwback and was as tough as tough can be. He was a gamer from the word go. He'd do anything asked of him."

Wedge came to the Cape after a successful season in the Great Lakes league and, like most college players, was hoping to improve his stock.

"I wanted to play in a wooden bat league and the Cape was the best for that," said Wedge.

"If you can hold your own in that league, you can make it. You're playing the best of the best and you get a true feeling for how good you are. It's a great barometer."

Wedge played in a summer which was loaded with future major league talent, including Jeff Bagwell, the long-time Houston Astros first baseman.

"You could tell Jeff Bagwell was going to be a special player," said Wedge. "He and I were drafted by the Red Sox the next year. I was third and he was fourth."

Wedge was taken by the Colorado Rockies in the expansion draft in 1993, but only played in nine games with the Rockies. He went back to Boston in 1994, playing in two games with the Sox before bouncing around in the minors for the next three seasons. "By 1997 I was done," he said. "I had knee and elbow problems." Wedge then turned to managing, and he was fortunate to have had a head start after playing for Reed, who compiled 334 Cape Cod league victories, eight first-place finishes and four league championships.

"Eric and I were very close," said Reed. "He and I would sit together during the rides and we'd talk about different philosophies. There were times he'd disagree with me and he'd do it in a nice way. He always wanted to learn more and I loved having him around. I like those guys who, if they don't understand why we're doing something, want to talk about it. He was one of those guys.

"He's the youngest manager in the major leagues now and he just has a wealth of knowledge. He worked his way up and he's very highly thought of."

JEFF BAGWELL

He probably doesn't realize it, but Jeff Bagwell helped a Chatham family become very involved in the Cape Cod league.

"When I became involved with the league in the late '80s, I had three daughters and a baby boy," said Peter Troy, president of the Chatham A's. "My two older girls were involved in softball and that seemed to bring me back into the baseball realm as their coach.

"Well, I was about that time I had heard of the Chatham A's then and I heard the players on that team ran a clinic. My oldest daughter, Casey, signed up. She loved it, and she got us going to the games. She kept talking about 'this kid Jeff.' She absolutely loved "this kid Jeff.' Well, 'this kid Jeff' was Jeff Bagwell and it was his second summer playing on the Cape. He was so good to my daughter and the next summer I signed up as a host family and I still do it."

In 1987, Bagwell came to Chatham out of the University of Hartford for the first of his two seasons in the Cape Cod Baseball

League. He captured the eyes of his peers, coaches, and scouts and was selected by the Boston Red Sox in the fourth round of the 1989 draft. He has distinguished himself as one of the top players in the game today, compiling a Hall of Fame career as a first baseman with the Houston Astros.

"The bat was swingin' him in '87," said Ace Adams, who was an assistant coach with the Chatham Athletics during Bagwell's first summer. "He was a very hard worker. He wore my ass out in BP. You couldn't throw enough BP to that guy."

Bagwell's intense work ethic carried over into the '88 season in his return trip to Chatham.

"Jeff Bagwell always, always had great hitting skills," said Bob Whalen, who managed the Athletics in 1988 and is the head baseball man at Dartmouth College. "He's the typical New England player. He always wanted extra work, always wanted to get better and always showed up early. We lost our catcher at the end of the season and he told me if I needed him to go back there, he'd do it. He's just a great kid."

As a third baseman, Bagwell more than held his own against the Cape leaguers, especially in his second stint with Chatham—a season in which he played against the likes of future major-leaguers Mo Vaughn, Chuck Knoblauch, Frank Thomas, Jeromy Burnitz, J.T. Snow and many, many more.

Statistically on the Cape, Bagwell didn't put up the big power numbers like he has in the big leagues, but he was certainly good enough to be selected among the top twenty players to travel to Florida to play in the Boardwalk & Baseball Tournament against other amateur summer leagues throughout the country.

"Bagwell was the best player on my team," Whalen said. "You knew his power was going to come, but no way did I know he would be what he is now. I'd be lying to you if I told you I knew he would hit 400 home runs in the majors. He made himself a player."

It was at the University of Hartford where Bagwell learned to become a complete hitter.

"Jeff was always a line-drive, pull hitter," said Dan Gooley,

Bagwell's coach at Hartford. "I credit everything about Jeff's development as a hitter to my assistant in Hartford, Mo Morehardt. The one thing he did with Jeff is made him realize there was a right-center field. He was a pull, pull, pull guy, but he learned to use the entire field. He was a power hitter in college but he learned to become a great hitter. He was extremely dedicated.

"From a physical standpoint, Jeff was in the strength room five out of seven days. I couldn't hit him enough ground balls. I couldn't throw him enough batting practice. The coaches were dead after working with this guy. His work ethic was unbelieveable. As far as a person, he is the salt of the earth. If you're going to have a son, you would like him to be like Jeff Bagwell—totally committed, worked hard all the time, just a first-class guy. He has never forgotten his roots."

Bagwell apparently hasn't forgotten his Cape Cod league roots either.

"When the Cape season was over, I wanted to get a game-used hat from one of the Chatham players," said Matt Hyde, who was the batboy for Chatham and is now the assistant baseball coach at Harvard University. "I didn't care who wore it, but I just wanted a hat used by a player. Jeff Bagwell threw his hat in the trash can and I immediately grabbed it. I asked Jeff sign it for me. That thing was so dirty, I had to keep in on the deck to air it out for about a week or so. My parents wouldn't let me bring it in the house.

"I remember in 1991 at Shea Stadium, the Astros were there and I had the hat with me. The signature was faded and Bagwell was being mobbed, but I made my way through with the hat. He saw me and said, "Matty, what are you doing here?" and he signed it again for me. After the game, I saw him again and he had his family and friends around. He saw me and I waved to him, and he came over to me and thanked me for coming. I still have the hat today and it still smells."

CAPE COD PROSPECTS
JEFF BAGWELL - 3B
CHATHAM A's

Jeff Bagwell spent two summers playing ball on Cape Cod and was a member of the 1988 all-star team, which featured a number of future big leaguers.

CORY SNYDER / JOEY BELLE

Cory Snyder arrived in Harwich in 1983 from Brigham Young University and left as the Cape Cod league's leading home run hitter—a record which still stands. Joey Belle came to the Cape for two seasons, playing in Chatham in 1986 and Hyannis in 1987, and left as one of the Cape's most feared hitters—a legacy which traveled with him through the big leagues. Both enjoyed double-digit years in Major League Baseball, with their careers peaking as members of the Cleveland Indians in the early '90s.

"The year before I played in the Cape Cod league, I played in the Alaska league," said Snyder, who was inducted into the Cape Cod league Hall of Fame in November of 2003. "I loved playing in the Alaska league, but I wanted to go back east to see the other talent out there and I also wanted to show myself to another part of the country.

"Playing in Alaska was fun, but it wasn't even close to the Cape as far as pure baseball excitement goes."

Snyder impressed many by smacking twenty-two home runs— the most ever by a Cape Cod player in one season. Using an aluminum bat, he is also the lone Cape player to hit three homers in one game twice in a season, and also smacked home runs in four consecutive at-bats.

Snyder said the two amateur leagues were on a par with each other, but gave a slight edge to the Cape when it came to recruiting talent.

"The leagues were very comparable," he said. "There was a lot more traveling in Alaska as the cities were a lot farther apart. The talent was also comparable, but I would say the Cape Cod league might have had a little better talent because most of the players in Alaska were from the West Coast and the Cape Cod league had people from all over.

"The people on Cape Cod take pride in their baseball programs. They really care about it. The atmosphere there is just incredible. It's full of emotion."

"I remember the game when we beat Wareham 6-2 and Cory

Snyder hit three two-run homers," said Steve Ring, who managed Snyder in 1983 and skippered the Mariners for five seasons.

"He was such a talented player. He was about twenty years old—but a very mature twenty—and had a very good head on his shoulders.

"I still keep in touch with him today and I'll tell you he is the same person today as he was twenty years ago."

Belle, Snyder's future teammate with the Cleveland Indians, racked up twelve home runs in his first season on the Cape. His numbers weren't as gaudy as Snyder's, mainly because Belle was forced to swing with wood after the league permanently made the switch from aluminum in the1985 season.

"Albert Belle was one of the hardest working guys we had on the Cape," said Don Reed, an assistant in Chatham during Belle's first season. "He was known as Joey back then. He came early every day. He asked me to come early and he worked extremely hard. All I did was sit there and put a ball on a hitting tee and watch him hit the heck out of the ball. Defensively, it was a different story, but his hitting was absolutely outstanding."

Belle's twelve homers still stand as a Chatham single-season record, and his 39 RBIs are fourth on the all-time A's list. Belle, according to Reed, was more than just a power hitter.

"He was a smart hitter," Reed said. "He was a very smart guy. He came from Shreveport, a big city, and I believe he was second in his class."

Ring recalls his favorite Belle moment on Cape Cod.

"He drove people crazy," Ring said. "He was playing for Chatham against us one year and I remember one particular at-bat. First pitch, strike. Second pitch, strike. Next thing you know, there's no batter in the box for the next pitch. He went back to the dugout. He just disappeared. The umpire went over to him to find out what the story was and he told the ump he was trying to regroup after those first two strikes."

WILL CLARK

When describing Will Clark, the sweet-swinging, left-handed first baseman out of Mississippi State, the word intense is likely to roll off the tongue quicker than any other adjective.

A few former Cape Cod league players have accused the league of taking summer baseball too seriously and abruptly packed their bags and headed back home. Clark's response to the walkout is simple and forthcoming.

"Hey, listen, if you don't want to take it seriously then don't come," he said. "Why go up there to play baseball and not take it seriously?"

"You could tell he was special from the time he got there," said George Greer, who managed Clark in Cotuit during that 1983 season. "He was the consummate team player. He was very intense and he wanted to win. He'd lay down a bunt if you needed him to. He'd play the outfield if he was asked."

To this day, Greer, the long-time head baseball man at Wake Forest University, continues to bring up Clark's name when talking hitters to his players.

"I always used him as an example when I talked about hitting the opposite way," Greer said. "He was a great hitter. He was very knowledgeable and picked things up right away. He was savvy, had a lot of intuition and was a real pleasure to have on the team."

Clark headed up to Massachusetts in 1983, and other than going off to school, it was his first time away from home for any significant time.

"I went up there not knowing anybody," Clark said, "but when I got there, there were two guys playing on the Cape who I played high school ball with—and they wound up being on my team up there. That made me feel a little more comfortable."

"Will Clark is easy to remember," said Arnold Mycock, the former GM of the Kettleers. "He was about 6-2, skinny kid with a high, squeaky voice. Intense is the best way to describe him. He was very, very focused."

Mike Govoni, who began hosting Cotuit players in 1983 and later went on to become vice president of the Kettleers at the end of that decade, said Clark also had a little bit of wit mixed into his personality.

"I remember telling him I never thought he would be able to play first base," said Govoni. "He said to me, 'Mr.G., I guess that's why you don't coach.'

"Will Clark showed up at my house one day and I asked him what his philosophy on the game was. He told me that baseball was one sport where if you're successful in three of ten times, you can be a hero. He had a great attitude and he came over the house quite a bit."

Clark suited up for the Kettleers and had a strong season, batting .367 with eleven doubles and ten home runs. Despite the lofty batting average (which, at the time, was the third highest in team history), Clark wasn't even the Kettleers' top hitter that summer.

"Greg Lotzar hit .414 for us that year," Mycock said. "He had sixty-three hits in forty games. He was also the base stealing champ with thirty-three."

Clark's stay on the Cape came two years before the league permanently switched to wooden bats. Clark, however, showed he could make the adjustment from aluminum to wood as he went on to spend fifteen quality years in the majors, finishing with a .304 lifetime batting average.

"Probably the worst part about having a pro career was not being able to go back to the Cape in the summertime," Clark said. "I thoroughly enjoyed my stay on Cape Cod.

"I knew a little about the league from guys on my college team who had gone up there before me. Back then, I think the Alaska league was probably considered the best summer league, but I thought the Cape was great. It was by far the best competition I played in at that point, and I played for Mississippi State in the SEC, which was also good competition. But in the Cape, you were playing against some of the best talent from all across the country."

Like those before him, Clark verbally passed the torch to the underclassmen at his school, suggesting they play on the Cape if given the opportunity.

"I passed it along to a few of the guys at Mississippi State," he said. "My brother (Scott) went and played up there."

According to Greer, Clark wasn't only at his best on the field.

"He was such a nice person," said Greer.

"I appreciate the fact he was very nice to my son when he was here. My son was about ten and was the batboy. Will went out of his way to be nice to him. He treated him like a person, wasn't just nice because he was the coach's son. To this day, my son speaks highly of him."

Clark said he has no regrets whatsoever about playing ball on Cape Cod, but wishes he could've made one change.

"The only thing I wish I could change about my time there would be I would've liked to play with the wooden bat," he said.

BRIAN ANDERSON

Brian Anderson is shown here in the summer of 1992 with Kay Britt, left, and Kay's daughter, Lisa. Brian steals carrots from Lisa's lunch.

It didn't take long for Kay Britt and Brian Anderson to strike up a relationship when the crafty left-handed pitcher spent two summers with the Wareham Gatemen.

Kay was the secretary for the Wareham Boosters Club and spent some of her time at the baseball clinics and working the snack bar. Brian was a young pitcher out of Wright State, whose summer job was working those clinics. He also made a few trips to grab a burger or two.

The two hit it off immediately, and although the Britts weren't Anderson's host family, Kay acted as his second mother.

"He was a guy working in the clinic, and I got to know most of the guys working there," Kay said. "Brian had an awesome personality. A lot of the guys there were very shy, but Brian was very outgoing. He said to me, 'boy, you're just like my mom.'"

He wasn't the only one to utter those words.

"His parents came here and we went to the games and went out to eat," said Kay, "and people would say I was so much like his mother. I guess it was because of the way we acted around our kids. We weren't afraid to give a hug or a kiss to them in front of everyone. I told his mother I would watch out for him."

Anderson stayed with different families in his two stints with the Gatemen, but always found time to stay close to the Britts, who had two young children and not much extra room to host a player.

"He would have liked to have lived with us his second season, but with two young children and a small house, we really didn't have the room," said Kay's husband Steve. "Still, we saw a lot of him. When his family visited, we went out to eat with them and we went to Brian's away games with them. When his girlfriend visited, he brought her to the house—almost as if to get Kay's seal of approval."

"After his second season, he came up to me and asked if he could stay with us for a week," Kay said. "He didn't want to go back home right away. He just asked if he could spend an extra week and we let him."

"Looking back, the experience actually prepared us for our own kids' teenage years," said Steve. "Brian introduced us to the old sleeping-in-until-noon trick. Kay would plan supper for him, and he wouldn't show—just like our kids are now. But he really was a joy to have around."

Like most of the young college players, Anderson was quite the all-around athlete when he arrived in Wareham. "The first year, he came late," Kay said. "He was trying out for the USA team. He drove all the way from Ohio and pitched that same night. He pitched a great game."

His talent wasn't limited to baseball.

"He was great with the kids, but not so great for my ego," said Steve. "I've always tried to stay in pretty decent shape, but in one game of touch football in the back yard, Brian put a juke on me and flew past me like I was tied to a tree. I was no match for a true athlete. Actually, I think it was a little emotionally scarring. I've never felt the same about myself since. After my hair loss, that little incident in the back yard probably did more damage to my fragile psyche than anything I can remember."

Kay says she still keeps tabs on Anderson, who has spent eleven seasons in the major leagues, and has taken trips to see him when he comes to Boston.

"One year when he was with the Angels," Kay said, "I went up to Fenway Park to see him. I saw him and shouted. He had such a look of surprise on his face. He was shocked and asked me what I was doing there. I told him I was surprising him. He said, 'no, I'm surprising you. I rented a car and I'm driving to your house after the game.'"

Anderson drove to the Britts' house on two occasions after playing at Fenway.

"The other time, I asked him if he wanted to go see some of the other people he met when he was playing here and he said he just really wanted to watch college football and have a pizza," Kay said.

The Britts were invited to Anderson's wedding, but because of a family medical emergency, they couldn't attend. As the years have passed, they have seen less and less of Anderson, but he did surprise them by sending them four tickets to the 1999 All-Star Game at Fenway.

"He's a great person," Kay said. "He's very polite and always had a sparkle in his eye. He is someone you hope your kids will grow up to be like."

CHARLIE NAGY

In 1987, a young pitcher out of the University of Connecticut had an opportunity to play summer baseball in Alaska, but with a little help from his college coach, Charlie Nagy decided to stay in New England.

Granted, UConn isn't one of the more high-profiled baseball schools across the country, but Andy Baylock, who had coached the Falmouth Commodores on the Cape in the mid-70s, wanted to give his player the chance to play in the elite summer league.

"(Baylock) had a few connections on the Cape and he talked to a few people and was able to get me there," said Nagy, who pitched in the big leagues for fourteen seasons. "Once I had the opportunity to go there, there was no temptation for me to go to Alaska.

"I sort of felt out of place at first, because I was with guys who I was reading about in *Baseball America* and everyone there showed up in their team garb and I just had on a t-shirt and some shorts. I didn't feel intimidated, though. Once I got over that little hurdle, I felt like I belonged there and I realized baseball was still baseball."

"I told Roger Lefrancois, who was the assistant coach then, you've got to give this kid an opportunity," Baylock said. "The Cape was at the point where it was tough to get a player there. They're going after the guys from Arizona and those big-time schools, and when you get a good one here, it's a challenge to get him in there.

"He had a great arm and he was a great competitor. He was very athletic and was also a very good football player."

Nagy pitched in the bullpen for the Harwich Mariners, who went on to capture the league championship. Nagy's teammates that season included future major-leaguers Bob Hamelin and John Flaherty.

Prior to his stint with the Mariners, Nagy had never pitched in a wooden-bat league, and admits he didn't give it much thought until he set foot on the Cape.

"I heard stories about throwing inside and sawing someone's bat off," he said, "and it was fun when I broke my first bat. I didn't think about it at all when I was in college. Wood is new to the hitters, too. When you break that first bat, you want to do it again."

Nagy was one of the very few Cape Cod players who didn't live with a host family. He, his girlfriend at the time, and her brother rented a small cottage in town. He did, however, maintain a league-issued job as most players do. He bagged groceries at the local grocery store in Harwich.

Playing on the Cape, Nagy says, was the most exposure he ever had as a player and was well aware of the many scouts who attended nearly every game.

"There was a ton of exposure that summer," Nagy said. "At UConn, I never really paid any attention to the scouts. On the Cape, you couldn't help notice all the guys behind home plate with their radar guns."

One of Baylock's fondest memories of Nagy happened outside the white lines.

"When Cleveland was playing the Red Sox in Boston during the playoffs, he called me and asked if me and Mama Bear—he called my wife Mama Bear—wanted to be his guests for the game," said Baylock. "I remember we went back to the hotel after the game and he and his wife Jackie and me and my wife, along with Brian Giles, who was one of his good friends, went out to dinner. We were walking through the streets of Boston and here he is, after just beating the Red Sox in the playoffs, walking in shorts, just being himself.

"He said to me, 'Jackie and I want to do something for the University of Connecticut.' He endowed a scholarship in their name. This is obviously something he didn't have to do, but that's the kind of person he is. He's a real class act and is as fine a person as I've ever met."

TIM SALMON

When Tim Salmon came to the Cape in 1988 from little-known Grand Canyon College and first set foot in Cotuit, he didn't exactly tear the cover off the ball. As the season wore on, however, the future Anaheim Angels outfielder heated up for the Kettleers and earned his way on to the Cape Cod league all-star team. His sudden resurgence can be attributed to two major factors—adjusting to his new surroundings and fear of failure.

"I have been a slow starter my whole life," Salmon said. "In the Cape, it was the first time that I almost was hurt by it. I thought I was going to be sent home.

"I think (early struggles) was a combination of a few things. Being away from home for the first time, tougher competition, unfamiliar coaches and surroundings, and, of course, the wood bats. The hardest part was finding a wood bat that felt comfortable. I remember grabbing a Pete Rose model that ended up being like thirty-five inches long and probably thirty-three ounces. That's a big difference from the 34/31 aluminum. In college, we would swing wood during batting practice but that was all."

Salmon credits Cotuit general manager Arnold Mycock with helping him stick around long enough to make the all-star team.

"I am grateful to him because he stood behind me when others were calling for my head," Salmon said. " I found out after the season that the slow start almost had me sent home. It was Arnold that kept me around long enough to get on track. You know, I sometimes wonder where I would be today had I been sent home that summer. I really do think he was one of those individuals that was instrumental to my success today."

"He did struggle early, but he came on like gangbusters," said Mycock. "We wouldn't send a kid home because of his performance—not in this league. When we sign up a kid, he's here to stay, unless there's a disciplinary reason or he leaves on his own. He came along great and was one of the nicest kids we had. He was a very soft-spoken, very conscientious, young man. He was a very good fielder—he had a tremendous arm—and he was fast for his size."

Salmon's struggles were evident by his .067 batting average on June 21, but his sudden resurgence lifted his average to .301 by August 1.

"Once he got used to the wooden bat, he was fine," said Mike Govoni, Salmon's host father. "One day he was sitting in the Jacuzzi and he told me he needed to apologize to me for his performance. He was down, and he was concerned, but he adjusted pretty well."

Salmon has gone on to enjoy a twelve-year major league career with the Anaheim Angels, yet he distinctly remembers his days playing ball as a teenager on the Cape. His memories of playing for the Kettleers hit full swing each time the Angels come to Fenway Park for their annual meeting with the Boston Red Sox.

"Every time I go to Boston I think about the Cape," Salmon said. "The Cape reshaped my thinking of baseball at the time. I was in my own little world out in Arizona, not realizing the world of talent and what baseball was all about on the East Coast. I became a Red Sox fan, following them that summer. I walked away admiring Dwight Evans and modeled my game after him.

"I saw the passion for the game through the people I met. I came away realizing more than ever that I, too, might become a major leaguer like so many other Kettleers before me. It was an honor to be associated with a team that had the history of the Kettleers. It was my first taste of playing big-time baseball. Remember, this is coming from a kid that played at a small school. I realize those that played at the D-1 schools might not have felt like that, but I did. I came home more mature and with a better focus of what I wanted to do and be. It really was a great stepping stone to professional baseball."

NOMAR GARCIAPARRA

Nomar came to Cape in 1993 and had a solid season for the Orleans Cardinals. Nomar was teammates with future big leaguers, Aaron Boone and Jay Payton.

The future Boston Red Sox and Chicago Cubs shortstop came to the Orleans Cardinals out of Georgia Tech in 1993 with some pretty lofty expectations.

"He came here with a great reputation, but matched everything that was said about him," said Rolando Casanova, who managed the Cardinals from 1991-1996.

He also came with a lot of hype.

"There was a lot of anticipation to see him because he was on the Olympic team the year before," said Casanova. "When the team reported, he wasn't there yet. We were getting ready to open against Harwich and we expected him to be there for the game. We're getting ready to play and he shows up. There was a reporter with a TV camera hounding him and you could tell he was very tired from the trip. I told him he didn't have to play and he said, 'I'm here. Where's my uniform?'

"When he was in the on-deck circle, there was a media guy with a camera and he was all over him, and when Nomar went up to bat for the first time, he laced the ball for a triple. I remember the TV guy runs over to third base and catches a shot of him as he slides in. I was thinking this is going to be a very interesting season. They all wanted to see him."

Garciaparra was also teamed with future major-leaguers Aaron Boone and Jay Payton that summer and the Cardinals went on to capture the Cape Cod league championship with a late-season surge.

"We were in third place with two games to go," said Dave Mitchell, treasurer of the Cardinals organization. "The real star that week was Jay Payton. We needed to win the last game to tie for second place, and Jay hit a home run in the ninth inning. We then had a tie-breaker against Brewster and he knocked in the winning run to put us in the playoffs."

While Payton provided the heroics that week, Garciaparra was quite consistent, supplying the fireworks for the season.

"I don't think Nomar hit a blooper all year," said Mitchell. "He hit so many line drives right at people and still hit about .325."

Garciaparra finished with a .327 average—good for seventh best in the league —and added 18 RBIs, 10 doubles and 17 stolen bases. He hit one home run.

"Nomar was the best player I ever threw to," said Falmouth's Jason Garman, a pitcher out of Princeton who made the 1993 all-star team. "I swear I couldn't get that guy out. I threw back-to-back starts against his team and I bet he went 5-for-7 or so against me. He hit one off me that I think is still going. One game I hit him in the head with a curve. The next time up, I threw a good curve and he drilled one right back at me and it was like he was trying to hit it off my head."

Despite Garciaparra's offensive statistics, defense was his game. He teamed with Boone at third base to form arguably the best left side of the infield in Cape Cod league history.

"Boone was a terrific third baseman," Mitchell said. "I don't think Nomar had to make a backhander all season. Boone was that good."

Garciaparra also had his share of outstanding plays in the field. One, in particular, took place in the late innings of that opener against Harwich and frustrated the Mariners. The frustration level also reached one of Garciaparra's teammates.

"I called him 'Gato,' meaning cat, because of his quickness," Casanova said. "We were up by a run late in that game and they had either two on or the bases loaded. A guy hits a rope to short and Nomar lunges—full extension—grabs the ball and throws the guy out. We had a utility infielder on the bench and I heard him yell 'shit' as Nomar made the play. He was upset because at that point he knew he wasn't going to be playing much."

According to Casanova and Mitchell, Garciaparra was just as strong an individual off the field.

"He was a very intense person," Casanova said. "He was very educated—just a very nice person."

"He was a delightful individual and I think that's something the Boston media didn't appreciate," Mitchell said. "He's still close to his host family and he calls them his East Coast mom and dad.

"I remember one time the wife of the assistant GM wanted to have a day for the kids from the May Institute (children with autism). All the guys on the team were there teaching hitting and fielding to the kids for about two, three hours. At the end of the day—and this is the stuff that sticks with you—there were about 40 youngsters around Nomar after many of the other players left. He was joking around with them, flipping the ball to them and they were having a great time. You should've seen the smiles on their faces. I have loved Nomar ever since that day. He was being very nice and very sincere to them. He is such a nice person."

UP AND COMERS

It takes talent, a little bit of luck, and the right situation to help a young college player reach his goal of playing baseball professionally. Nobody understands that more than *Mike Bynum*.

Bynum, a southpaw who earned a pair of late-season call-ups with the San Diego Padres in the 2002 and 2003 seasons, wasn't too familiar with the Cape Cod league when he was hurling for the University of North Carolina.

"I didn't know much about the league at all," Bynum said. "I know my college coach wanted me to play summer ball and I knew it was one of the best summer leagues, but that was about it."

Bynum enjoyed two fine summers with the Hyannis Mets after struggling with the Tar Heels. In fact, his second summer on the Cape was so good, he was selected as the starting pitcher in the 1998 all-star game, ahead of Barry Zito and Ben Sheets.

"Those guys are having pretty good major league careers so it was a pretty good accomplishment for me," said Bynum. "I had horrible college statistics—they weren't good at all, but I had two good years in the Cape league and was noticed by a few scouts."

Those scouts liked him enough to make him a first-round pick—the 19th overall selection in the 1999 draft, which also consisted of Zito (10th overall) and Sheets (11th).

"I knew I wanted to play pro ball and the Cape league is definitely good preparation for it," Bynum said. "This was the first time I dealt with wooden bats, and those years were pretty much my first time away from home. Using the wood bats, playing every day is exactly what we're doing now. Back then I found it pretty wearing, but I have gotten used to it. Playing baseball is what I really wanted to do, and I was having success so I didn't get burned out at all. I really believe I wouldn't have made it if I didn't play in the Cape league."

Todd Linden, a young outfielder with the San Francisco Giants who earned a late-season promotion to the big leagues in 2003 when Barry Bonds took time off following the death of his father, enjoyed a solid 2000 Cape season after being snubbed by Team USA—a collection of the nation's top collegiate players who tour the country and other parts of the world throughout the summer.

"There was some talk about me playing for Team USA, but for some reason or another it didn't work out," said Linden, who was drafted by the Giants as a supplemental first-round pick in 2001. "Scouts have told me it worked out for the best because I had a better opportunity playing in the Cape Cod league.

"It's a little more of a pride thing, playing for Team USA," said Brad Grant, the Cleveland Indians assistant director of scouting, "but the Cape Cod league plays better competition than Team USA does."

"I had talks with other leagues, but playing in the Cape Cod league was my number one priority at the time," Linden said. "I had a blast playing there. I remember it was a very mild summer and it was just a beautiful place to play. It was very relaxing and a great environment. Playing there opened the door for me. It gave me some great exposure, but it wasn't high pressure."

Russ Adams, like Bynum, attended North Carolina and also didn't do much of a background check on the Cape Cod league before playing for Orleans in 2001.

"An assistant coach at North Carolina got me a spot up there," said Adams, and infielder with the New Haven Ravens (Toronto Blue Jays Double-A affiliate). "Coaches want to get their players to play summer ball and that's the league where they start. Going in, I didn't know a whole lot about the Cape league, I just kind of showed up."

Adams was a first-round selection of the Blue Jays (14th pick overall) in 2002, and was a key member of the Ravens, who fell to the Akron Aeros in the Eastern League Championship in 2003. He made his major league debut with the Blue Jays in 2004. He remembers his time spent in New England as a learning experience both on and off the field.

"It was my first time being up North. I had played in the Coastal Plains league in Durham the year before, and I'm from North Carolina. The Coastal Plains league is a very good league, but most people think the Cape Cod league is the best and I'm definitely one of those people. It's really an experience all college players want to have. It's a good tool for preparing players for the minors.

"It was a great atmosphere up there. I played for Orleans and I think they led the league in attendance. Everyone on the Cape is so close to each other, and the league is very comparable to pro ball. It definitely helped me prepare for what I'm going through now."

Another infielder who was a first-round pick and should climb the minor league ladder quickly is *Drew Meyer*, who spent two seasons (2000, 2001) playing in Chatham.

Selected four picks ahead of Adams as Texas Rangers' top pick, Meyer thrived on the competition and accepted the challenge of having to learn to make the adjustments to the wooden bats.

"It was my first time using wooden bats for an extended period of time," said Meyer, who finished the 2003 season as a member of the Frisco Rough Riders (Double-A, Texas) and hit .316 in 26 games. "It was actually kind of fun using them. You had to learn how to make adjustments."

According to John Schiffner, his coach at Chatham, Meyer adjusted very well and has a pretty healthy professional career ahead of him.

"Drew Meyer is the best shortstop I've seen in the Cape Cod League," said Schiffner, who has been involved in the CCBL for 30 years as a player, scout and manager. "I think I can say that without pissing people off. You just took the great plays he made in the field for granted. He'd go up the middle, do a 360, throw on the run and get the guy out by a couple of feet and you'd just say, 'yup, good play,

Drew.' You can see he's a good hitter, the power is there, and he's got speed like Secretariat. He's a flat out, five-tool player."

While he was having a blast between the white lines, Meyer also was having a good time when he wasn't playing ball.

"Chatham is such a great town," he said. "I'd go to the beach a lot and I really enjoyed that. I'm from South Carolina and the summers are usually very hot, so it was a nice change.

"The league is great because it brings in a lot of scouts. It works both ways because the scouts are also able to see the nation's talent. It worked out well for me because the right scout saw me, and I'm very happy with the way things are going."

Pat Misch, a left-handed pitcher out of Western Michigan, came to play for Falmouth in 2001 and 2002 not knowing what to expect. He left with one of the best experiences of his life.

"Those two summers were probably the best summer of my life," said Misch, a seventh-round draft pick of the San Francisco Giants in 2003. "No, not probably, those were definitely the best summers of my life.

"I went there after my sophomore year from Western Michigan. A scout from the Marlins called the coach at Western and asked me if I wanted to play in the Cape. I think I drove out there the next day."

As a youngster, Misch was always into baseball, but never thought he would one day make the trek to the Northeast, especially for the sole purpose of playing the game he loved.

"I'm from Chicago and when I was a little kid, I looked at Massachusetts, Connecticut as little states and wondered why the heck I would ever go up there," Misch said. "But I got a chance to go to Martha's Vineyard and Nantucket and it was just awesome. Being surrounded by the ocean and the great weather, you can't beat it. I definitely plan on going back there to visit.

"As for baseball, scouts are there all the time, the competition is great. I certainly had to take advantage of that opportunity. I told all the younger guys back at school to work hard and do what they can to go there and play."

When *Joey Metropolous* came to the Cape from USC in 2003, he admits he wasn't all too familiar with the league either, but he arrived in the right frame of mind. He had no expectations, put no added pressure on himself and just went up there to play ball.

"Baseball is a failing game anyway," said Metropolous, who arrived on the Cape after his sophomore season. "If you fail seven out of ten times at the plate, you're a good hitter. You just have to fight through the times when things aren't going well."

Like most, Metropolous struggled a bit, but the power-hitting first baseman earned Cape Cod league all-star honors by smacking eleven home runs for the Falmouth Commodores.

"I definitely struggled and I can honestly say I just happened to hit a hot streak," Metropolous said. "I was the Coca-Cola Hitter of the Week one week when I hit four or five home runs. So out of the eleven home runs I hit, I hit almost half of them in a week. I was seeing the ball real well at that time."

Metropolous wasn't overwhelmed by the abundance of scouts in the stands, simply because he was accustomed to their presence at highly regarded USC. Scouts certainly knew of Metropolous, who was a ninth-round pick by the Toronto Blue Jays in 2004, but he never felt any added heat playing in front of them.

"I didn't really find there to be too much pressure. There were a lot of scouts there, but at USC, there are always scouts there, too. The only reason there might be some pressure was because this was the summer before my junior season and this could be my last summer playing. I felt if I went out there and played my game, I'd be ok. I didn't want to go out there and get too focused on feeling I had to play well every night. I just wanted to go out there and be myself."

Metropolous also said playing on the Cape was similar to playing back home in California, except for a couple of minor details.

"It's pretty much the same as it is here in California," he said. "The only difference was it got a little foggier and there were more a lot more mosquitoes. I made a few good friends while I was out there and the clam chowder was unbelievable."

Metropolous was also selected to take part in the home-run-hitting contest in the all-star game, which was won by Vanderbilt's

Cesar Nicolas, a power-hitting first baseman who was spending his second summer on the Cape.

Nicolas played a key role on the Orleans team which came away with the 2003 Cape title, and he says his experience of having played for Harwich in 2002 helped him succeed the following season.

"The first summer, I did struggle at first," Nicolas said. "Before you go there for the first time, there's a lot of hype. You realize you're playing against the best players in the country. Most guys, like me, are timid and overwhelmed right away. Then I realized I was there for a reason and I held my own."

Nicolas more than held his own as he was named to the all-star team and finished second in the home-run contest.

In his second season on the Cape, Nicolas knew what to expect in the league and was ahead in the game when it came to making adjustments at the plate.

"Playing in the Cape, you learn how to make adjustments with the wooden bat," he said. "There's a significant difference between wood and aluminum, but the difference isn't in the bats, it's in the swing and the mechanics. There's so much less room for error with wood and you learn to make those adjustments."

"Cesar is a power hitter and he's capable of big power," said Vanderbilt head coach Tim Corbin. "But he's really an atypical power hitter because he's got a very good line-drive stroke. A lot of power guys have flaws in their swing as they try to get under the ball too much, but Cesar has a good idea of how to drive the ball."

Nicolas emerged as the winner of the home-run-hitting contest in his second season, but certainly didn't let the title go to his head.

"In the grand scheme of things, it doesn't mean that much," said Nicolas, chosen in the fifth round by the Arizona Diamondbacks in 2004. "But it meant a lot to me. It was an honor to go up against all those great hitters. It was a lot of fun to be a part of that. I'm very grateful to have been able to go up there and play. You learn so much about the game and you also learn about being independent. You mature a lot as a person. Those two summers I spent up there are irreplaceable."

Just because you don't come from a big-time Division-1 baseball school like Metropolous and Nicolas, doesn't mean you can't succeed against the big boys on the Cape.

Arriving from Division 2 University of Tampa, *Eric Beattie* was arguably the premier pitcher on the Cape in 2003, compiling fantasy-like numbers while pitching for the Bourne Braves. Beattie was 4-0 as a starter and recorded fifty-one strikeouts in forty-six innings pitched, while walking six. His ERA was 0.39 and his numbers were good enough to earn him the BFC Whitehouse Award, an award given to the league's most outstanding pitcher.

His success on the Cape undoubtedly played a key role in making him the Detroit Tigers' second-round pick in 2004.

"Coming to the Cape was a huge question for me," said Beattie, entering his junior season at Tampa. "I had no idea if I would be outplayed coming from a D-2 school. I really didn't know anything about the Cape league. Sam (Militello, the UT pitching coach) gave me some paperwork before my sophomore season and gave me a little background and I went."

Militello played for the Falmouth Commodores in 1989 and spent the 1992 and 1993 seasons pitching for the New York Yankees.

Beattie's Tampa teammate Wally Quigg also helped the six-foot-three right-hander feel right at home—literally—when he made his trip to New England.

"Wally's from Bourne," Beattie said. "I was fortunate I was able to stay with his parents when I went up there. It was my first time being away from home and the Quiggs were just awesome. They made it fun for me and I don't know what it would've been like if I didn't stay with them."

Coming from Tampa, Beattie is used to playing baseball year round, yet he welcomed the chance to play another five or six days a week against the top college prospects.

"I wasn't burned out at all," he said. "I played something like 110 games in five months or so and I loved it. Some guys I know dread going to practice, but I loved it. I just love playing baseball."

If *Matt Murton* continues to play like he did for the Wareham

Gatemen and maintains the same attitude he's always had, the first-round pick of the Boston Red Sox in 2003 will go a long way.

Never one to focus on his own numbers, Murton could very well be impressed by his own statistics, but chooses to look at baseball in the team concept.

"The two summers there were successful," said Murton, an outfielder out of Georgia Tech. "I was fortunate to have a great group of people around me and was put in the best possible situation to succeed."

"Perhaps the greatest player I have ever met in the Cape league is Matt Murton," said Sean Walsh, the GM of the Bourne Braves. "There is an aura about him that spreads to his teammates that makes one know his team will win. I have seen him hit a 94-mile-per-hour fastball with an 0-2 count and two outs in the bottom of the ninth with fans screaming and shouting and everything on the line. His smile is infectious. He makes you feel at ease. He is approachable and as genuine a man as I have ever met."

He was also pretty good at making adjustments.

While using the wooden bat for the first time for a full season, Murton was the Cape Cod league's MVP in 2001 after leading the league in RBIs with 28 while finishing second in batting average at .324.

"Using the wood was good in a lot of ways," said Murton, who was dealt, along with fellow Cape Cod league grad, Nomar Garciaparra, to the Chicago Cubs at the 2004 trading deadline. "With aluminum, so many guys just swing for the fences. With wood, you have to shorten your swing and put the good part of the bat on the ball. Adjustments do have to be made and you have to swing correctly."

Murton rejoined the Gatemen in the middle of the 2002 season after breaking his finger during a Team USA tryout in Tucson that summer. He returned to the Cape with a bang, winning the home run-hitting contest during the all-star game festivities, and leading the Gatemen to their second straight league title.

"The biggest thing I noticed about the Cape was how much pure baseball it is," Murton said. "The sound of a wooden bats is so much sweeter than aluminum. You don't play on the best fields and there aren't 25,000 people in the stands. It's just pure baseball.

"What the Cape Cod league did for me as far as getting to pro ball was great. I went to Georgia Tech and that was great, too, but the Cape really set me up for pro ball."

While most players come from college and see their offensive numbers drop significantly when they come to the Cape, the opposite held true for Louisiana State University's *J.C. Holt*, who arrived in Brewster for the 2003 season.

"I've always hit about 20 points higher with wood," said Holt, who played second base and center field for the Whitecaps. "I don't know what it is. When I went up there, I made a few changes in my swing, but nothing real major. I struggled my sophomore year and going to the Cape was kind of a way for me to start over."

Struggling for Holt, a third-round selection of the Atlanta Braves in the 2004 draft, meant hitting .300 in his second season at LSU, but that came after batting .353 as a freshman.

After his freshman season, he played in a wooden-bat summer league in Danville, Illinois, and racked up a .368 batting average.

"When I went to the Cape, my goal was to hit over .300," he said. "I figured if I could hit somewhere between .300 and .320 against that pitching, it's be a great summer."

Holt surpassed his wildest expectations by finishing with a .388 batting average, securing the batting title in the process and walking away as the league's MVP. Holt's batting average is the best since Wareham's Mark Smith hit .408 in 1990.

"At one point, I had a chance to reach .400," he said. "I was at .391 and had a 22-game hit streak and the next game I was 0-for-1 with a walk and the game was rained out in the fifth."

Holt's success can be attributed to hard work and a lot of hitting. He was one of the few players who didn't hold a job during his three-month stay.

"I woke up at eight every morning and went to the gym for about an hour and a half," he said. "I was always out there hitting early. I didn't work because I didn't want to get distracted."

Holt had always been an infielder, switching between second base and shortstop, but his college coach moved him to center field to utilize his speed. When he came to the Cape, he played eleven games at second base and the rest in center field.

"I think playing both positions can only help me," Holt said. "I've talked to several scouts and half tell me they like me at second and the other half tell me they like me better in the outfield. Where I play doesn't matter to me."

Could Holt duplicate his season and hit .388 if he came back to Cape Cod for a second summer?

"I don't know if I could do that again," he said. "I think I'd give it a run—maybe .350. I've never hit under .350 before, except for my sophomore year."

Chapter 2
Scouting

"What the Cape Cod league does is brings the college player back to reality. A lot of these guys come here and find out they're not as successful with the wooden bats."
–Stan Meek, Florida Marlins scouting director

"It really was an eye-opener for me. It was a humbling experience playing with the wood bats. I hit .250 with no home runs. I did well in college, and playing up in the Cape league was really the first time I had struggled, and it taught me how to deal with struggling."
–Todd Sears, Falmouth '96

If there are any members of a scouting team who know the ins and outs of the Cape Cod league, it's Deric Ladnier and Stan Meek.

Ladnier, the senior director of scouting for the Kansas City Royals, was an all-star third baseman for the Falmouth Commodores in 1984, the year his all-star squad suited up against that high-profiled Olympic team, featuring Mark McGwire, Will Clark, Cory Snyder and several other future major-leaguers.

"That was a summer I'll never forget," Ladnier said. "Playing against great competition and against the Olympic team are the things you remember."

Ladnier was an eighth-round pick by the Royals in 1985 and his career was cut short after making his way to Double-A.

"I was blessed with injuries," he said.

Now, instead of playing with the guys on the field, he's in charge of those who get paid to watch them play.

"The Cape Cod league gives scouts an opportunity to evaluate good college players, many of them are potential draft picks," he said. "The level of competition is great. They have all been invited to play in the Cape league for a reason. Playing there makes you a better player."

Meek, the scouting director for the Florida Marlins, was the manager for the Wareham Gatemen in the 1986 and 1988 seasons, and was named the league's top skipper during his second summer.

Playing summer ball on the Cape is all about learning to make adjustments, and many scouts pay more attention to how the players fine-tune themselves rather than their statistics.

"Looking at their numbers helps," said Meek, "but you don't walk away from a player if he doesn't hit.

"We watch them during batting practice because we're able to get a feel for their bat speed. You've got to have some strength to swing wood."

One player who grabbed the scouts' attention was Tim Salmon, out of Grand Canyon College. Salmon came to the Cape in 1988, playing for the Cotuit Kettleers, and going up against the likes of Mo Vaughn, Frank Thomas, Jeff Bagwell, Chuck Knoblauch in the Cape year which arguably produced the best major-league talent. Salmon held his own against that strong group of Division-1 talent, making the all-star team and watching his confidence soar in the process.

"I didn't know who those guys were at the time," Salmon said. "Call it naïve, but back then the only players I knew about were the ones from Arizona. I will say that it ended up being the best level of play other than the big leagues.

"I was drafted out of high school and followed pretty closely in college my first year. As a freshman, we went to the NAIA World Series and that increased my value. But all the scouts were encouraged by my performance in the Cape. It definitely jumped me up some notches in their eyes."

While Ladnier and Meek were a part of Cape Cod Baseball in the 1980s, scouts Lenny Merullo and Bill Enos had CCBL roots long before.

After an eight-year career with the Chicago Cubs as a shortstop from 1941-1948, Merullo began working for the Cubs in 1950 as an area scout, covering baseball throughout New England. He worked for his former major-league team until 1973, when the Major League Scouting Bureau began, and then was employed by the bureau for the next thirty years.

Prior to his big-league ball, Merullo had already established a relationship with the Cape Cod Baseball League, playing with the Barnstable team in 1935. His two sons also participated in the league, along with his grandson, Matt, who was a catcher in the majors for six seasons.

"When we looked at players, we had a few different classifications," Merullo said. "We started with franchise player. Then we had definite players, meaning he'd be a major league player, but not necessarily a can't-miss player. We then had prospects and organizational players. After you've been scouting a while, you can tell who's going to be a player immediately, just by the way he walks onto the field. He'll attract your attention right away. Then you start to break him down with the positives and negatives.

"When a player is recommended to play in the Cape league, we already have reports on him in the computer. We go in believing every player in the Cape league is a prospect. We always go in with a positive attitude."

Merullo says he also keeps tabs on the players who have traveled through Cape Cod.

"I got to know a lot of the ballplayers who went through the Cape and made it to the majors," said Merullo. "They're like family to me. When I'm looking at players today, in my mind I'm thinking, 'I saw him at Orleans' or 'I saw him at Chatham.' There are some guys who you don't think will make it, but they surprise you."

Merullo still follows pro baseball, following the team for which he played.

"I'm a Cubs fan for life," he said. "Once a Cub, always a Cub. I was a weak-hitting, erratic shortstop, and you can look me up in the major-league record book for making the most errors in an inning. I made four in one inning. That's almost impossible. It happened the day my son was born. He's sixty-two now and they still call him 'Bootsie.'"

Enos also had a taste of pro ball, managing in the St. Louis Browns organization in 1949, but later became the link between Major League Baseball and the Cape Cod league.

"It was back when Bobby Brown became president of Major League Baseball when I was appointed as the liaison," Enos said. "Major League Baseball was supporting the Cape league financially, so I had to make sure the league was cooperating. I had to write up reports. Everyone involved in the league was very cooperative, and the people who run the Cape are all volunteers so I wasn't about to run up to them and say do this, do that. I recommended a few things and they were very cooperative."

Enos has spent sixty-six years in baseball, signing with Rochester at the age of sixteen, and insists times have changed, but the game hasn't.

"Back when I managed in the minors in late '40s, I had to coach, I had to play, and I had to drive the bus," he said. "We only had a fourteen or fifteen-man roster and we played 140 games. "As far as the scouting changes, up until 1965 when the draft was initiated, scouts could go into the Cape and sign players right away. People keep saying the game is changing, but it hasn't changed at all. You still have to get three outs and there are still nine players in the field."

Enos, who was responsible for signing John Tudor out of Falmouth, says the Cape Cod league is a great way for a player to get noticed, even if he doesn't end up getting drafted. He also admitted scouts aren't always correct on their judgment of players.

"The Cape is a great league for a fella to play in, and if you aspire to play pro ball, you can't find a better place," Enos said. "About four or five years ago, there was a pitcher in the Cape who went 7-0 or 7-1 out of Tulane. He wasn't drafted and he was discouraged. I told him I thought he could pitch and gave him a shot. He's in the majors now—Jack Cressend.

"Scouts do make mistakes. Many scouts only tell you about the good players they signed, you never hear about the guys who don't pan out."

For a good percentage of the players in the CCBL, it is the first time they've experienced playing with the wooden bats for an extended period of time, and it becomes a rude awakening for many.

"It really was an eye-opener for me," said Todd Sears of the San Diego Padres, who played for the Falmouth Commodores in 1996. "It was a humbling experience playing with the wood bats. I hit .250 with no home runs. I did well in college, and playing up in the Cape league was really the first time I had struggled, and it taught me how to deal with struggling."

"It's not a tell-tale sign but it gives us an idea that if a guy has a lot of success in the Cape league, playing with wood, the chances his transition to pro ball will be easier," Ladnier said.

"What the Cape Cod league does is brings the college player back to reality," Meek said. "A lot of these guys come here and find out they're not as successful with the wooden bats."

Cleveland Indians third baseman Casey Blake is one of those guys.

Blake struggled mightily during his time with the Hyannis Mets in 1993, but has worked his way up the professional baseball ladder and has solidified his place in the major leagues with better-than-average numbers.

"It was my first wooden-bat experience and I remember in my first game I had a real good swing and hit a dribbler down the line and just said, 'oh man, I've got to get used to swingin' this lumber,'" said Blake. "I didn't play as well as I wanted to. I think I ended up hitting something like .205."

Mark Snipp, the Toronto Blue Jays former assistant director of scouting, signed Blake out of Wichita State in 1996.

"Casey struggled at Wichita state, too, a little bit, but he's very athletic," Snipp said. "One of the adjustments he had to make was changing his swing. I think the guy who is credited with helping him change is Ernie Whitt."

Like Blake and a host of others, Baltimore Orioles second baseman, Brian Roberts, had a tough time adjusting to swinging wood when he played for the Chatham Athletics in 1998.

"It's definitely tough for anyone to make that switch from

aluminum," said Roberts, whose father, Mike, coached the Wareham Gatemen in the 1984 and 2000 seasons and came back to coach the Cotuit club in 2004. "Of course, I struggled, but there aren't too many who don't. You go through a lot of frustration, but you try not to let it discourage you. But you seem to get frustrated no matter what. The scouts realize what you're going through—they understand it, but I didn't."

Despite Roberts' frustrations at the plate, he insists learning to deal with his struggles helped him become a first-round pick of the Orioles in 1999.

"Playing up there helped me a lot," he said. "I went up there after my sophomore year, and when I returned to school I knew what I had to work on. Despite the frustrations, it really was the best summer I've ever had playing baseball. Now that I've gone there, I can see how it helps you both as a player and a person."

"What I see about guys today is that most of them grew up with aluminum bats," Snipp said. "They have an aluminum-bat swing. When they come to play here on the Cape, one of the first things I look for is to see if they're able to make the adjustment to the wooden bats."

As difficult as it is for the hitters to amend their batting techniques, the pitchers also have to make some adjustments when it comes to facing the wooden bats. The one major change pitchers are forced to make is learning to throw inside, which can often result in a sawed-off bat and an easy out.

"I don't care what you do as a pitcher, you have to throw inside," Snipp said. "I don't care if you throw 80, throw inside."

"I loved pitching in the Cape league," said Oakland Athletics pitcher, Barry Zito, who pitched for Wareham for two summers. "It gave me the opportunity to pitch in an all-wooden-bat league and get a feel for what that was like."

Pat Misch, a seventh-round draft pick of the San Francisco Giants in 2003 and a two-time member of the Falmouth Commodores, adjusted to this logic quickly.

"When you throw inside at college, it can still be a base hit," said Misch, who attended Western Michigan. "When you throw inside with a wood, it's a broken bat. I'd say the Cape league is a pitcher-dominant league, but you still have to pitch to your strength, work hard, and hit your spots."

Misch also used a little bit of his own logic.

"These guys are struggling a little bit with the wood bats so you kind of let the hitters get themselves out," he said.

"We look at the mentality of the pitcher while we're up here," Meek said. "We see if he'll pitch inside. When you're using an aluminum bat, pitchers tend to pitch away, they try to miss the bat. When they're up here using wood, we look for their aggressiveness."

"The sweet spot on the aluminum bat is pretty much from the handle all the way to the top," said former Oakland Athletics all-star catcher Terry Steinbach, who was the CCBL's batting champ while playing for Cotuit in 1982. "But with wood, it's probably 3-4 inches."

According to Chris Buckley, the Jays' former director of scouting and now a special assistant to the GM in Toronto, the Cape Cod league is a prime tool to help get ready for pro ball, but statistics can be misleading.

"As scouts, we put a lot of stock in this league," he said. "Some kids will definitely struggle here. Craig Biggio hit .200. Lance Berkman never hit a home run there. Sometimes you have to look beyond the numbers."

Berkman actually finished with one home run for the Wareham Gatemen in the summer of 1996, but the lack of power certainly didn't get him discouraged.

"I won the batting title," said Berkman, who finished with a .352 batting average, "and I'd rather win the batting title than hit six or seven home runs up there. I've always hit home runs, but that one year I just hit one. I'm sure going from aluminum to wood played a part in it, but you also get only 200 or so at-bats. Hitting that one home run didn't bother me one bit. I think the scouts took it harder than I did. They said that was a knock on me, but I didn't let that bother me because most of the scouts never played the game. I knew I hit .350 and was hitting the ball hard."

"It's so hard to tell how good a player is by his numbers," said Jim Higgins, the senior vice president of the Cape Cod Baseball League, who sees between fifty and sixty games each season. "Lance Berkman and Todd Helton combined for one home run when they were here—and Berkman's hit the foul pole."

While Helton was shut out in the long-ball department for the Orleans Cardinals in 1994, he, according to his coach, did it intentionally.

"Todd Helton was the cockiest, most confident SOB," said Rolando Casanova, the manager of the Cardinals in 1994 and now a scout with the Detroit Tigers. "I called him 'Biggen.' It was really 'Big One' but he was from the South, so I ran it together and made it one word—Biggen. He thought he could walk on water.

"He had no homers, but he was hitting over .300 with a bunch of doubles. The all-star game was right around the corner, and I told him if he really wanted to get noticed, he had to show some more juice. If he didn't show any juice, he was going to be a player like Mark Grace—a good player with not much pop. He said, 'Coach, I have a lot of juice. I've just been working on my gap hitting.' I just kind of nodded my head as if to say, 'yeah, right.' Well, he took part in the home run-hitting contest and hit seven of the first ten pitches out of the park. I guess he was telling me the truth."

"It's very difficult to predict how far these players will go because of their physical makeup," Higgins said. "When Nomar (Garciaparra) was here, he was about one hundred and forty pounds. When you saw Mo Vaughn, Frank Thomas, you're seeing players in their developmental stages. You'd never think in your wildest dreams that they'd grow up to be what they are.

"There are also guys like Mike Bordick and Jeff Reardon who both went undrafted. Pro scouts got a chance to look at Jeff Reardon for three seasons and they didn't draft him."

The Cape Cod league is beneficial to virtually every scout, but the Blue Jays seem to get a little more out of it, simply because of their approach.

"This league is good for us because ever since (general manager)

J.P. Ricciardi has been here, the emphasis has been on college players," Snipp said. "That's his M.O. He stresses the college guys."

As beneficial it is for players to participate in the CCBL, scouts are quick to point out the league is also advantageous to them. Not only are they able to see the country's elite college talent, they can do so without a grueling traveling schedule.

"I get to see two games a night," Snipp said. "I don't get to see two full games, but the towns are close enough where I can leave one game and go pick up another."

"We try to see every pitcher and every position player," said Steve Fleming, a sixteen-year veteran of the Pittsburgh Pirates scouting team. "You can't always do that, but you get to see some of the best college talent in the country. It's a great league and the people involved in it take it to heart. They do a great job running the league and it's really a fun place to be for the scouts, too."

"I make it a point to go up there every year," said Meek. "If I didn't, my wife might not stay with me."

Chapter 3

The Host Families

"John Wasdin was a sweetheart—still is. He has three lovely daughters and we're the Cape Cod grandparents. He's a wonderful human being and gets along with everyone. I remember he wanted to be called Juan Wasdinez because he thought it would get him farther in baseball."
–Mary Anne Lynch, host parent

"Mike (Govoni) was home all the time from a work injury, so he basically became our host mom. He did everything. Breakfast would always be waiting for us in the morning with a newspaper, and dinner would be served at the time appropriate to accommodate our game time in the evening. The Govonis were a good family and I'm thankful for their hospitality."
–Tim Salmon, Cotuit '88

There's a whole lot more to the Cape Cod Baseball League than what takes place on the diamond. Just as important as the success of a player's performance on the field is what happens off it. Many long-term relationships have been built between the players and the families who are willing to host a player (or players) during their summer stay. For many Cape players, it's their first extended time away from home, without living in a dorm, and not only are they learning to deal with unfamiliar places and new faces, they have to cope with sharing a house with strangers ready to open their doors to them. During their stay on the Cape, most players work a job, set up by the league, and are required to use a portion of that money to pay rent to their host family.

Dave Sauro began hosting Cape Cod league players from the Hyannis Mets in the late '80s and became so involved in the league, he became the president/GM of the Mets for four years.

"I don't know exactly how I got involved as a host family, but I remember we saw an ad in the newspaper and thought we'd give it a shot. We had an in-law apartment, had three young daughters, ranging from ages seven to thirteen, and the girls enjoyed it," he said. "I thought it would be nice for my girls to have a brother for a couple of months."

In 1988, the Sauros hosted a young player out of Oklahoma State by the name of Jeromy Burnitz, who bonded real well with the family, laying the groundwork for a long-lasting connection.

"Jeromy became a family fixture. He even came with us on family trips to New Hampshire. Of all the players we hosted, he's the one who really became a part of our family. He just kind of fit in. He occasionally would go out with the guys on the team, but usually on the days he didn't have a game, he pretty much did what we did."

Jill Sauro, the oldest of Dave and Janice's three daughters, was thirteen at the time, but clearly remembers Jeromy's energetic personality.

"He was quite the character," she said. "I remember he pulled up in his bright orange BMW with his foot hanging out the window and I said to myself, 'Who's this dude staying with us this summer?'

"He was a great guy. He was eighteen or nineteen and was our big brother. He'd take us skating in the summer and he'd fall asleep in the stands watching us."

Burnitz has gone on to play eleven seasons in the big leagues and happened to be a participant in the 1999 All-Star Game's Home Run Derby contest at Fenway Park.

"I went up there to see him that night and I met him outside the clubhouse after the contest," Dave said. "In fact, that night he missed the team bus and we had to give him a ride back to the hotel."

One theory why they hit it off so well is because Burnitz was the lone player staying with them that season. The Sauros were supposed to host Burnitz and Mitch Simons, his college teammate, that year, but Simons got hurt and went home, leaving Burnitz as the lone non-Sauro living in the house.

Another presumption for the strong relationship involves water.

"One thing Jeromy enjoyed was the water," Dave said. "I think that was one connection we established with him. He really enjoyed water sports.

"As much as he loved the water, his dedication was to baseball—the sport that brought out his serious side.

"Jeromy was also a serious kid, and we joked about it. We had a T-ball set up in the back yard, the kind where the ball was attached to a string and would come back to you, and whenever Jeromy had a bad game, he'd go into the yard and you'd hear 'whack', 'whack' and we'd just look at each other and say, 'Jeromy's at it again.'"

"I remember during his games he would be out there talking to himself out in right field," Jill said. "When he didn't do well hitting, he'd go out there and talk to himself or talk to the fence.

"We had a great time with him. The girls really loved him. He had his little groupies out there and we'd tease him about it."

For the Sauros, baseball became a family event. While dad was running the Mets, mom was busy cooking and baking for the team, Jill and her sister, Lauren, were handing out 50/50 raffle tickets at the games, and seven-year-old Maia was being picked on.

"The players were always teasing her," said Jill of the youngest Sauro. "They had a blast with her."

The Sauros also hosted major league catcher Doug Mirabelli one season, and during Dave's time as general manager, he got to know Jason Varitek, who was the catcher for Hyannis in the 1991 and 1993 seasons.

"Jason Varitek, not only did he have talent, his attitude was great," Sauro added. "I don't know if there's a better person out there. And that's one thing I found out about my experience with the Cape Cod league—in addition to these kids being very good college ballplayers, they are outstanding people, too. Like they say on those (Mastercard) commercials, the memories I have of being involved in the league are priceless."

If anyone on the Cape knows the true character of Jason Varitek, it's Kelly King, whose family hosted the Boston Red Sox catcher during his two summers in Hyannis.

In his second season, Varitek arrived in Hyannis well after the 1993 Cape season had started after electing not to sign with the Minnesota Twins, who made the Georgia Tech junior catcher their No. 1 draft (21st overall selection) pick that year.

"People were saying he was making a big mistake by going back to school," King said. "They were saying he put up such impressive numbers in 1993 that he wouldn't be able to do it again. They said he wouldn't be able to improve his draft position since he was already a first-round pick, and they said he would have no leverage as a senior."

Varitek called King after turning down the Twins and asked her if she thought the Hyannis Mets were interested in having him back for another year.

"I said, 'Jason, are you crazy? Of course, they'd love to have you," King said. "I think he flew out here the next day."

Varitek's decision to put off playing professionally paid off, especially for the King family, as he was the first-round selection of the Seattle Mariners in 1994 (14th overall) and eventually traded, along with Derek Lowe, to the Boston Red Sox for Heathcliff Slocumb in 1997.

"I was so happy when he was traded," King recalled. "I called the Pawtucket Red Sox that night to ask when he would be here, and they said, 'He's coming tomorrow.' We packed up the kids and went to the next game.

"I put a recipe for clam chowder, his favorite, on the front of a postcard with the words "WE'RE HERE" on it, and I had someone put it in front of his locker. He came out looking for us. At the end of the game, he was still looking for us. He finally saw my daughter and he had a big smile on his face. We ended up eating dinner with him, and we'd go up to Pawtucket just about every night after that."

The relationship Varitek and King developed through the years continued to grow so much that when Varitek was inducted into the Cape Cod Baseball League Hall of Fame in 2002, the Red Sox catcher asked his host mother to present him at the ceremony.

"I knew Jason was going to be inducted because I had spoken to (league president) Judy Scarafile," King said. "She said to me, 'maybe he'll ask you to present him.' I said, 'yeah right.'

"Then one day he called me and asked me if I would, and I said, 'Jason, can't you pick someone else?' He said, 'yes, but I want you to do it.'"

King was very flattered to speak for her friend at the Chatham Bars Inn that November night, but also felt a bit awkward at the ceremony.

"I felt very much out of my element," she recalled. "Ron Darling was there, Peter Gammons was there, and there I was."

While other induction speakers glanced over their notes that night as they delivered their speech, King went up to the podium and spoke from the heart.

"I didn't have any notes," she said. "I knew what I wanted to say. I wanted to give my personal side.

"I spoke about the ups and downs Jason had as a nineteen-year-old freshman. I spoke about how he became a part of our family, and how much of a pleasure it was to watch him grow. I also said Seattle made one of the biggest mistakes ever by trading him."

The audience that night was captivated by King's speech, and those in attendance included Jason and his wife, Karen.

The Variteks made the trek to the Cape that night, despite the fact Jason's father had undergone open-heart surgery that week.

"That's the kind of person Jason is," King said. "He made the commitment to come here and he did. Once he knew his father was going to be ok, he packed up and came right up here."

King also recalls the impact Karen had on Jason prior to their marriage.

"When he came here in '91, he didn't know her," King said. "When he was here in '93, he had met her that spring. You could tell by the look on his face when he was talking to her on the phone that she was the one, and the rest is history.

"He married someone very special—she's such a sweetheart. She went to UGA (University of Georgia) and he went to Georgia Tech—arch rivals—yet she passed up her graduation in 1994 to see him play in the College World Series."

An avid baseball fan, King even attended spring training in Florida one year and made it a point to go see Varitek play against an old Cape Cod buddy—Pat Burrell of the Philadelphia Phillies—who was also a friend of King's from his days in Hyannis in '96.

"I told Jason to tell Pat I was here," King remembers. "After the game, I went over to the Philadelphia side where they were boarding the bus and I saw Pat there signing some baseballs. He was close to me and I just said, 'Pat Burrrrrelllll.'

"He said, 'I see you standing over there.' I asked him if Jason passed the message along and he said that Jason told him right when he went up to bat—and he ended up striking out."

King, her husband Chuck, and their four children, began hosting players in June of 1989 and continued for eleven summers. One of her wildest memories as a host parent was when a temporary player, Mike Terceira, came to stay with her family one summer.

"I said to Mike, 'Gee your last name is the same as my husband's aunt's,'" King said. "He said he didn't think so, that it was probably spelled differently. Then I asked him if he was related to Frank and Lucy, and his eyes lit up and he said he was. Here I was hosting a relative and I didn't even know it."

King says her family keeps in touch with about eighty percent of the players they have hosted through the years. They have been invited to weddings, receive annual Christmas cards, and some of the players even have come back for a visit.

Despite all the friendships King has made through the Cape Cod league, it's Varitek who seems to have made the strongest impact.

"There's not a week that we don't talk," King said. "He is such a well-rounded person. He's very polite and he's so bloody humble. Honestly, he won't talk about himself. He has always managed to turn it around and get the spotlight off him and put it on someone else. He's a great dad, a wonderful person. He's just very genuine."

Not too far from where the Kings reside, lives another family that hosted Cape Cod players for more than a decade. Jim and Marianna Lynch took in multiple players per season beginning in the summer of 1990, which started as a trial period.

"We had two young boys, so we kicked the idea around," Jim said. "We decided we'd give it a shot to see if our boys enjoyed it."

Apparently, the boys liked it to the point where the Lynch family became regulars when it came to providing college players with a place to stay. During their tenure, they hosted future major-leaguers John Wasdin, Brian Buchanan, Carlton Loewer, and Randy Choate.

"We had a great time with them," Jim said, "but the only one we really stay in contact with is John."

"John Wasdin was a sweetheart—still is," Marianna said. "He has three lovely daughters and we're the Cape Cod grandparents.

"He's a wonderful human being and gets along with everyone. I remember he wanted to be called Juan Wasdinez because he thought it would get him farther in baseball."

The Lynches exemplify what the Cape Cod Baseball League is all about. They fully admit they're not huge baseball fans, but still volunteer their services, as evidenced by the fact Marianna was once the head of housing for the Hyannis Mets.

"My wife is definitely not a baseball fan," Jim said. "She couldn't even tell you the color of a baseball, but she was very involved."

The Lynch family would support their guests by attending nearly every one of their baseball games, whether it was in Hyannis or on the road. Although, while in the crowd, you wouldn't find them with a scorebook, charting pitches or figuring out batting averages. It did, however, matter who came out on top.

"Going to a baseball game was a social event for me," Marianna said. "It was, however, a whole lot nicer if the Mets won because everyone would be much happier when they got home."

Marianna keeps files with phone numbers, hometowns, colleges of the players she hosted, and the memories of her guests are as vivid as ever.

"Carlton Loewer was very quiet," she said. "He was gigantic. He did a lot of running and he was always dripping with sweat.

"Randy Choate talked so fast and talked a lot. Within an hour of meeting him, we knew everything about him. When he pulled up in his car, I couldn't believe it. His car was packed as if he was staying here permanently.

"Brian Buchanan, it was a very intense time with him. His parents were back and forth up here for negotiations with the Yankees. I distinctly remember him saying he felt like a piece of meat when he was here."

Sometimes an extra room or two, combined with a little luck, can turn even a non-baseball fan into a casual one.

Take Sam Francis, for example.

Francis hosted players from the Wareham Gatemen for a few seasons mainly because he had some extra living space and enjoyed the companionship.

"I had some spare rooms, I knew John (Wylde, the Wareham president/GM) and I was living alone so I thought I'd take in some players," Francis said. "It's good company.

"I never really liked baseball. I mean I don't dislike it, but I just wasn't interested in it that much."

During the 1988 season, Francis hosted two players, who would later go on to combine for more than 11,000 career major league at-bats.

Mo Vaughn and Chuck Knoblauch lived with Francis in his Marion home that year—his last as a host—and the two gave him a reason to follow baseball.

"I went to all their games when they were here," he said. "Mo's mom and dad, and Chuck's family came by a few times and we'd go to the games together.

"I'm an oddball. I'm not a baseball fan except when the players are friends of mine."

Vaughn and Francis already had an existing relationship from the previous year as the slugger had stayed with Francis in the 1987 season. Even before that year, the two had an ironic connection unknown to both of them.

"My sister had actually taught Mo in school a few years back," Francis said, "but I didn't discover that until Mo had been with me the first year."

Vaughn was a big, power-hitting first baseman, and Knoblauch was a speedy infielder, but their differences didn't stop with their size.

"The interesting thing to me is that Mo and Chuck were very different from each other," said Francis. "Mo was very laid back, happy-go-lucky. He really wanted to be selected by a major league team, but the whole summer he was really relaxed about it.

"Chuck was very intense. He was also a great kid, but he was very focused. He knew what he wanted and he was going to work like hell to get it. Nothing against Mo, but Chuck was more mature. People didn't know Chuck as much as Mo. Mo was more high-profiled."

The one similarity they did share was the fact they were still teenagers.

"I remember they came in one day with this huge flag they stole (from a local school)," he said. "This flag was so big. I told them they had to go bring it back. They ended up bringing it back, but they hid it so nobody knew it was them who took it."

On the nights the team wasn't playing, many of the Gatemen players would head over to Francis' house for a little food and some relaxation.

"When they were staying here, the team would come by quite a bit," he said. "We'd have some pizza, listen to music, watch television. I had a hi-fi system and we'd just hang around here.

"I had a wonderful career as an engineer. Mo and Chuck were interested in that and we talked about that a lot. We were interested in each other's careers. Theirs is interesting to me because it's totally different than what I'm used to. Career-wise, they have a limited life span."

Vaughn and Knoblauch made such an impression on the non-baseball fan that Francis even took the trip to Fenway Park when Vaughn and the Red Sox hosted Knoblauch's Minnesota Twins.

"I'd go up there to see them," he said. "I even sat with Mo's mother once or twice at a game.

"They were really great guys to be around, they worked very hard, and I was glad to have their company."

CAPE COD PROSPECTS
MAURICE VAUGHN - 1B
WAREHAM GATEMEN

CAPE COD PROSPECTS
CHUCK KNOBLAUCH - SS
WAREHAM GATEMEN

Mo Vaughn and Chuck Knoblauch were teammates and roommates in Wareham during the 1988 season.

Back in 1994, another non-baseball enthusiast decided to give hosting a shot, and now is she not only a fan of the sport, she has gone on to become president of the Bourne Braves.

Lynn Ladetto was "coerced" into housing players by a friend of hers during the summer of '94 and was immediately hooked.

"I loved everything about it," said Ladetto, who went from hosting players, to being in charge of fund-raising to becoming the president of the Braves. "Just watching the expressions on these kids' faces just changed it all for me. It made me realize how important baseball was to them and that's what really did it for me.

"I was not a big fan of baseball at all. I didn't really know anything about it. I couldn't have told you what a 6-4-3 double play was."

Ladetto's first player was Chad Schroeder, a pitcher from Northwestern now out of baseball, and that experience had a domino effect on her future as a host parent.

"As soon as we had Chad, I was hooked," she said. "We still keep in touch. Actually, we still keep in touch with just about everyone—some more than others."

Lynn and her husband Ed hosted up to as many as four players in one summer, and in 1996, the Ladettos took in Chicago Cubs second baseman Jerry Hairston Jr.

"Jerry was so dedicated," Lynn said. "Absolutely dedicated. He knew where he wanted to go and he was determined to get there. He still has that drive. He got along with everyone and fit in with my family and was very good with my son Kevin, who was eight at the time."

To this day, Ladetto keeps hold of one unique piece of baseball memorabilia from her housing days.

"Jerry worked at Stop & Shop in the produce department and I still have his autographed Stop & Shop hat and his pin that says J. Hairston," she said.

Lynn also credits the closeness of the community with helping her want to climb the Cape Cod league administrative ladder.

"The people in the community do a lot of volunteer work, which brings everyone closer together," she said. "It's a lot of work, but when you see everyone coming together, it makes it 110 percent well worth it.

"It's amazing so many people open their hearts and their homes to these kids. It can form very strong relationships. I know whenever Mark Mulder comes back to play in Boston, he always leaves four tickets to his host family."

When the Brewster Whitecaps began their inaugural season in 1988, Mark and Anne Sullivan caught Cape Cod Baseball League fever and decided to open their door to players on the local team. Little did they know, it would become a tradition that would span fourteen years.

In the Sullivans' initial summer hosting players, they happened to take in little-known Dave Staton out of Orange Coast College. Staton, however, quickly made a name for himself on the baseball field, smacking a wooden-bat record for homers and narrowly missing the Triple Crown on the final day of the season.

At six-foot-four and two-hundred and fifty pounds, Staton smacked sixteen home runs, putting on quite a power display in front of the faithful fans on the Cape. Back home, however, the Sullivans got a unique, behind-the-scenes look at another powerful side to the Brewster first baseman.

"You would always be able to tell if Dave had a good game or a bad game," said Mark. "We had two one-hundred-pound dogs at the time and if Dave had a good game, he'd pick up one under each arm and walk around the house. If he had a bad game, he kept pretty quiet. He didn't really show much negative emotion, but you'd be able to tell he didn't have a great game."

Chances are, the dogs' paws didn't spend much time touching the floor as Staton left the Sullivans' house as the Cape Cod league MVP that season.

"When he was on the field, he was one hundred percent focused," Mark said. "You'd walk by, wave and say hello and he wouldn't even notice."

Staton admits he had never heard of the Cape Cod league until the opportunity to play there was presented to him, and despite the unfamiliarity with his surroundings, he and the Sullivans hit it off right away.

"We connected on the first day," Mark said. "My wife and I don't have any kids of our own, but he was like one of ours. We treated all of them like we would treat our own. We played cards three or four times a week, played ping-pong together and went to the beach together. Dave didn't have a car and his roommate didn't have one either so we spent a lot of time together."

"My host family was nothing short of outstanding," said Staton, a California Highway Patrol officer who remains in contact with the Sullivans. "I thought so much of them when I was there. I still do. They told me we were the first players they hosted and it's because of us, they decided to do it again."

Anne says since it was the first time they hosted players, the level of nervousness was initially a bit on the high side.

"I think we were all nervous," Anne said. "He was the first one to come through our door, but after a few days we were used to each other. He made it very easy for us."

Anne also believes Staton's success on the field was a direct result of his will-do-whatever-it-takes-to-succeed philosophy.

"Everything was black and white with him," Anne said, "there was no gray area. Whatever he set out to do, he did. I remember driving home on Route 137 one day and I saw this guy riding a bike that was about five times too small for him. He had golf clubs on his shoulder. I looked back and said, 'Oh my God, it's Dave.' He was riding one of our bikes. He wanted to go golfing, he didn't have a car and was going to do whatever it took to golf."

When Staton left the Cape and went on to play professionally in the San Diego Padres organization, the Sullivans continued to follow his career.

"He had a great minor league career," Mark said. " In Las Vegas he has the longest home run ever hit. He went on to play in the big leagues.

"Some guys have big egos, but not Dave. He's very down to earth. He has a lot of integrity. He's very respectful and he had great parents. His whole family was very nice."

The Sullivans have also hosted a couple of other players who have reached the big leagues, including Tony Perez's son, Eduardo, and Roger Bailey.

"We've had many ballplayers and we keep in touch with a lot of them—some more than others," Mark said.

"In fourteen years of hosting players, we never had a problem," said Anne. "We had a few interesting experiences, but no problems."

When it came to hosting Cape Cod Baseball League players for the summer, nobody had a better set up than Sue and Chris Makepeace of Wareham.

"We owned a bed and breakfast in Wareham and my wife ran that while I stayed at the house with the players," said Chris, who, along with his wife, hosted players for three summers. "We would let the parents of the players stay at the bed and breakfast when they came up to see their sons."

During the three-year run as a host family, the Makepeaces were fortunate to take in players who were all respectful and polite. One of those players was Houston Astros outfielder, Lance Berkman.

"Lance just loved to play baseball," Chris Makepeace said. "He was deceitfully fast, hit from both sides and he learned a lot from Coach (Don) Reed."

The future National League all-star fit in nicely with the Makepeaces, and despite his well-mannered behavior, Berkman, according to Makepeace, wasn't quite up to par when it came to handling his laundry situation.

"His parents showed up at the Cape Cod league all-star game that year and his mother was so embarrassed with his laundry technique," Makepeace said. "He just had two piles of dirty clothes in his room and he basically just let them air out. He just did a sniff test and if they smelled ok, he'd wear them again. I remember his mother being so embarrassed with that.

"Lance was very polite—they all were. They were all family-oriented kids. Their parents were wonderful people, too."

While the players were well behaved, Makepeace says he still had to be strict with the rules when the team got together after a game.

"I live on a pond, and downstairs we have a pool table and my house always seemed to be party central after games," he said. "I had to put the hammer down a few times. The guys would be playing poker games well into the night and I'd have to tell them to tone it down every once in a while. I also told them not to bring any women over either or else I'd get in trouble."

Makepeace also loved to cook, and his desire to play chef came in very handy because Berkman had two other roommates, Brad Winget out of Brigham Young University and Jeff Andra from Oklahoma, staying with him that summer.

"There were three that year, and they were three big boys," Makepeace said. "I had to spend about three hundred dollars worth of groceries on these guys a week. (Wareham general manager) John Wylde would take them out to Papa Ginos or something after a game, then these guys would come home and I'd still cook for them—and they'd still eat."

"Now that you look back on it, you feel bad they spent so much money on us," said Winget, who spent two summers on the Cape—but only one year with the Makepeaces. "We went through cereal like crazy.

"I'll be honest, the host families make a big difference in your stay. The first year I was there, I stayed with a family and it was pretty much a nightmare. I was very lucky to be set up with the Makepeaces in my second year."

He was lucky in more way than one. He was fortunate the Makepeaces were the kind family they were and also lucky they decided to take in another body.

The Makepeaces were only scheduled to take in two players that season, and Berkman and Adam Kennedy were set to room together.

"If my memory serves me correctly, Adam got hurt at the end of his college season and there was some question about him playing here," said Wylde. "It was agreed that we would take him off our roster because of the uncertainty of the injury. His dad contacted us about halfway through the season and said he was ready to play, but the only spot we could've give him was in the outfield because we were all set in the infield. He went on to play for Falmouth that season and they were league champions."

Chris Makepeace also recalls the first year his family hosted players when Eric Gillespe (Cal State Northridge) and Clint Bryant (Texas Tech) stayed with him.

"One night I heard a lot of screaming and banging in the middle of the night, which was very unusual for those guys," said Makepeace. "I got up and went to see what was going on and they both had baseball bats and tennis racquets in their hands. I had no idea what was going on. They were both screaming and swatting at this bat in the house. They were acting like two ten-year-old girls. I had to go over there, open the door and shoo the bat out while they were screaming and hiding in the corner. I got a good laugh out of that one.

"I absolutely had a blast hosting the players. They were old enough to take care of themselves and they were very respectful."

When you've been hosting families for double-digit summers in the Cape Cod Baseball League, there's a pretty good chance you'll have taken in a future major-league player or two. Or three. Or four.

Mike and Judy Govoni began taking in Cotuit players in 1983 and capped their tenure as a host family in 1994 before packing their bags and moving to Florida.

During that eleven-year stretch, the Govonis were fortunate to have played the summer parental role to players such as Tim Salmon, Scott Erickson, Damon Buford, and Darren Bragg.

"We got involved because we had four boys of our own and they were very interested in sports," said Mike, who became the vice president of the Kettleers in the late '80s and held that post for three years. "It gave them an opportunity to have an older-brother relationship with them."

Of the four big leaguers, Salmon is the most known and came to the Govonis house in 1988 as a little-known outfielder from Grand Canyon College.

"Tim was a very quiet young man," Mike said. "He struggled when he was here, but he was very dedicated. He was very dedicated to the game and dedicated to his girlfriend Marci, who is now his wife.

"He also loved tuna fish. I remember he would always buy big cans of tuna. He was always eating that stuff."

According to Salmon, the Govonis were the ideal host family, making sure the players were fed and their uniforms were washed.

"Mike was home all the time from a work injury, so he basically became our host mom," Salmon said. "He did everything. Breakfast would always be waiting for us in the morning with a newspaper, and dinner would be served at the time appropriate to accommodate our game time in the evening. The Govonis were a good family and I'm thankful for their hospitality."

"I hurt my back at work and was home," Mike said. "Those were our boys for the summer and we treated them like they were part of the family. I always asked them if they wanted to eat before or after the game and had something ready for them. I also had to do their laundry because if they ever used the washing machine, their uniforms would turn pink.

"I remember one day Tim was hollering upstairs, 'where's my jock?' I told him that was not part of my job description."

Mike also has his stories about the others he hosted.

"Damon Buford was a strange creature," he laughed. "He was struggling here and he asked his dad (Don Buford, ten-year major-leaguer with the White Sox and Orioles) what he should do. His father told him to change things around and Damon took him literally. He did things like turning his entire bedroom around. I think he probably carried it too far.

"Darren Bragg would be late for his own funeral. He worked for my wife when he was here and he was never on time. He was such a loveable kid, though, and you just couldn't get mad at him. He was a guy if you wanted him to be somewhere at eight, you'd have to tell him 7:45 and maybe he'd make it.

"Scott Erickson was only here for two or three weeks. He was negotiating a major-league contract and was playing here while that was going on. He had a little bit of an attitude. The scouts even seemed to baby him a bit. They would call and ask for Scott and say, 'if he's sleeping, please don't wake him. We'll call him later.' After he signed his contract, it would be like, 'could you cook me some hot dogs, please?'"

The Govonis also became close with another soon-to-be major-leaguer, even though he didn't stay with them.

"Greg Vaughn was one heck of a nice kid," Mike said. "He didn't stay here, but spent a lot of time here because we hosted a friend of his, Ronnie Marigny from Tulane. Greg was a big boy and would just hop in the back of my truck and sprawl out.

"He was a very mild-mannered kid, but I remember being at a game where he just blew up and was thrown out of the game. He ripped off his shirt and went and sat in the stands. The umpire told him he had to leave the park and he said he couldn't go home until his host parents left. People in the stands were laughing at that one.

"I also remember the time when Greg and Ronnie met two stewardesses at the beach. I had always told them not to wake me up by coming in late at night. They ended up sleeping in the woods behind the house. When my wife left for work, they came in through the back sliders, and I was sitting there. They just gave me a look as if to say, 'uh oh, we got caught.'"

Like the Govonis, Bruce Murphy and his wife hosted players

from Cotuit for double-digit seasons, and like Mike, Bruce also took a front-office position with Kettleers, becoming the vice president of the team in 1989.

Unlike the Govonis, however, the Murphys only hosted one player who spent time in the majors.

Eric Valent came to play ball on Cape Cod in 1996 and then was a first-round pick of the Philadelphia Phillies in 1988. In between, he was a guest of the Murphys.

"Eric was very health conscious," said Bruce, who has been the Kettleers' general manager since 1999. "He would always go running around the block and he would jump rope a lot. He taught my daughter how to jump rope."

Even though there weren't many future big-leaguers staying at the Murphy house, Bruce did have off-the-field contact with several soon-to-be stars.

"Mike Matheny stayed at a house close to ours and he'd come over maybe two nights a week," he said. "He had this little-kid scooter and he'd ride it over and would play street hockey with my son.

"Lou Merloni would also come over to play some pool quite often. He was a very good pool player."

Murphy, a self-admitted sports nut, says he never took in players to see how far they would take their professional careers, but he enjoyed the little things that came with opening the doors to his home to a total stranger.

"I think the interesting part is getting to know the players," he said. "What do they like to eat? Little things like that. We had a kid from Missouri one year who had never seen the ocean before. His mother told him to make sure he got some pictures of seagulls when he was here."

Murphy does remember the on-the-field performances of some of the former Cotuit players who went on to play big-league ball.

"Bo Hart played for us and he didn't really do too much with us," Murphy said. "He may have hit around .280 or so, but sometimes we don't catch the kids at their peak. Aaron Harang threw for us, but we didn't get many innings out of him. He had flashes of brilliance, but

I would say he wasn't on top of his game most of the time. He was a big, thick kid. David McCarty could really hit the heck out of the ball, Josh Paul was a very upbeat, high-energy guy and Kirk Saarloos was a real free spirit with a nasty slider. Mark Bellhorn spent about two weeks with us and then went with Team USA. He left his car here and it stayed here about four months."

"But I'll tell you, Mike Buddie was probably the funniest kid we ever had. It was just one one-liner after another. You never knew how serious he was taking his time here. He was a great, funny kid who brought a bunch of laughs with him the whole summer."

According to Mike Govoni, Tim Salmon was dedicated to baseball and his girlfriend, Marci, who later became his wife.

Sometimes the off-the-field relationships developed in the CCBL can even carry beyond the player and the host family.

Drew Meyer, the No. 1 draft pick by the Texas Rangers in 2002 (10th overall) played two seasons for the Chatham Athletics, and stayed with the same family both seasons.

Suzanne and Roger Horne of Chatham took in Meyer for both summers during their two-year stint as a host family.

"We had two boys who were very interested in baseball, and we just thought it would be nice to host a player from the league," Suzanne said.

Meyer was sent to stay with the Horne's because he was one of the late arrivals as his South Carolina team was participating in the College World Series.

"The spring is a very busy time for us, so we asked if we could have one of the last players to arrive stay with us," said Suzanne.

That request paid off as Meyer and the Hornes hit it off immediately, but little did they know the tables would soon be turned.

Not only did the Hornes connect with Drew, but they also developed a strong rapport with the Meyer family.

"We built up a relationship with Drew's family," Suzanne said. "They came up here and we really hit it off. One day Drew's dad called and asked us if (our son) Greg would be interested in playing in an AAU tourney league down in Charleston (SC). They invited him to come and stay with him."

"My host family was great," said Meyer. "It was really my first time up north and the Hornes were very nice people and made me feel at home. We bonded real well."

Without hosting a Cape Cod league player, Greg wouldn't have had the unique opportunity to experience baseball life outside of Massachusetts at the age of sixteen, and the Hornes wouldn't have had the friendship with the Meyers.

"I think it's wonderful because it gives my son an opportunity to play in a whole different setting," Suzanne said. "It's his first time away from home, and he's playing on a team Drew used to play for.

"Drew's a family-oriented kid. He has all the qualities I see in my own kids. He's dedicated, compassionate, and great with young kids. He's just a great kid.

"The whole thing was a great experience for me. I think it brings a lot of families closer together and it helps build long-term relationships. We hosted one year for the experience, but Drew came back for another season so we decided to do it again."

Chapter 4

That Special Season

*"We wanted to use wood while the other teams used aluminum—
it was a matter of pride. Me and Jesse Levis were the catchers, Mo
(Vaughn) was at first, Chuck Knoblauch at short, (Jeff) Bagwell at
third and Tim Salmon in right. Frank Thomas and J.T. Snow didn't
even make the team."*

–Eric Wedge ('88 Yarmouth-Dennis), on the 1988 Cape Cod
league all-star team which won the Boardwalk & Baseball
Tournament in Florida despite being the only team to use wooden
bats.

When it comes to producing quality big-league talent, the Cape
Cod Class of 1988 is second to none. Frank Thomas and J.T. Snow
played for the Orleans Cardinals, Mo Vaughn and Chuck Knoblauch
were teammates in Wareham, Tim Salmon and Dan Wilson laced
'em up in Cotuit, Jeromy Burnitz played in Hyannis and Jeff Bagwell
was manning third base in Chatham.

Other 1988 players such as Mike Mordecai (Yarmouth-Dennis),
Steve Parris (Yarmouth-Dennis), Denny Neagle (Yarmouth-
Dennis), Eric Wedge (Yarmouth-Dennis), Mark Johnson (Bourne),
F.P. Santangelo (Brewster), Craig Paquette (Brewster), Mike Myers
(Brewster), Mark Sweeney (Chatham), Mike Trombley (Falmouth)
and John Valentin (Hyannis) also enjoyed healthy major-league
careers.

The crop of players that summer was so good, a twenty-player all-
star team was assembled and traveled to Florida for a Boardwalk &
Baseball Tournament, a double-elimination, four-team round robin.
The Cape stars were the only team to use wooden bats in the tourney
and still managed to secure the title. After losing the opener to the
Great Lakes league, the Cape team earned five straight victories,
highlighted by a Salmon two-run home run on the final day to help
seal the championship.

"Mo Vaughn and I were friends and I remember going out to dinner with him after we lost the first game, saying there was no way we're going to lose again," said Wedge, the catcher on that squad and currently the manager for the Cleveland Indians.

"We wanted to use wood while the other teams used aluminum—it was a matter of pride. Me and Jesse Levis were the catchers, Mo was at first, Chuck Knoblauch at short, Bagwell at third and Tim Salmon in right. Frank Thomas and J.T. Snow didn't even make the team."

"The list of the guys who didn't make the team is almost as impressive," said Stan Meek, the 1988 Manager of the Year out of Wareham, who skippered that all-star squad. "You had guys like Frank Thomas, J.T. Snow, John Valentin, and Mike Mordecai.

"The guys we did have were amazing. We had three guys, Knoblauch ('91), Salmon ('93) and Bagwell ('91) who went on to be Rookies of the Year in the majors."

"We had a lot of good players during my time there (1982-1991) and it apexed in 1988," said John Castleberry, who coached the Orleans Cardinals and is now a scout with the Texas Rangers. "It seemed like every team that year had a dude—a big-time future major-leaguer."

The loss in the tournament opener was tough, but some of the players took it a lot harder than others.

"For us, it was really a no-win situation," said Castleberry, one of Meek's assistants in Florida. "Even though we used wood, we were still supposed to win. People expected us to win. In the first loss, they were getting a lot of bleeder hits against us. I know we made a few errors—Bagwell made a few. They were tough plays, but they were errors and it may have cost us two or three runs, but then again he was throwing to Mo, who was about as agile as a light pole. I remember walking with Eric Wedge to the hotel and he was telling me Bags was crying. He took it hard."

The loss to the Great Lakes league eventually proved to be a blessing in disguise for the Cape leaguers.

"The Great Lakes team was very cocky after that opening win," said Meek, now the scouting director for the Florida Marlins. "They were saying how they had just beaten the mighty Cape. Our guys were very competitive and they were basically harassed by the Great Lakes team. They laughed at us and that didn't sit very well with our guys. After that game, I told the guys that I didn't know if we would win the tournament, but I wanted to win enough games to play them again. I told them whether we win the whole thing is immaterial, but let's just win enough games to get one more shot at those guys. They bought into that and it fired them up. That team made a mistake by popping off to us."

"The Great Lakes league was selling itself as a great league," said Castleberry. "They were very cocky. They were razzing me when I was out there coaching first base. They were also supposed to be using wood in that tournament. There were supposed to be two teams using wood and two teams using aluminum. They chickened out."

The unexpected loss also brought the use of the wooden bats into question for the Cape leaguers.

"I remember Fred Ebbett (former Cape Cod league commissioner) and a few others came up to me after the game and said maybe we should consider using aluminum," Meek said. "I told them there was no way I was going to make that change. We had come down here to make a point."

The point was well made as the Cape team earned four straight victories and set up Salmon's heroics in the rematch with the Great Lakes league.

"I remember my home run only because I didn't hit many that summer," Salmon said.

Coming from a very small school, Grand Canyon College, Salmon was honored to be on the same team with all that future major-league talent.

"It was great to be associated with that bunch of all-stars," he said. "By then I knew them and what they could do. Also, it was a boost to my own confidence because I knew what the scouts were saying about them, and I figured I wasn't that far behind some of those guys as far as talent went. That tourney was great, but I remember thinking we were the best team before it ever started. Everyone wanted to be in the Cape, so I assumed we had the best players in the country. I really didn't know much about the other leagues."

"Tim Salmon had the liveliest bat in the league," Meek said. "The ball just jumped off his bat. He was a misser sometimes, but when he hit the ball, it just jumped off the bat.

"It was nice to go back and beat those guys, especially using wood while they used aluminum. That was almost like playing with one hand tied behind your back, but we went out and made a statement."

The Cape all-stars actually had to defeat the Great Lakes league twice that final day to secure the title.

"We beat them the first time," Castleberry said, "but then we had to play again right away. Actually, we agreed to play a seven-inning game because we both had flights to catch."

The Cape leaguers held a comfortable three-run lead late in the nightcap and brought in Chatham's Michael LeBlanc, out of the University of Maine.

"I remember he walked someone," Castleberry recalled, "and then it was something like double, single, double and before you knew it it's a one-run game. It all happened so fast. I remember Stan turned around to me and (assistant) Don Reed and said, 'I thought you said this guy can pitch.'

"Down one, they were trying to bunt the tying run over with nobody out. The batter missed and couldn't get the guy over. (LeBlanc) had a heck of a slider and he regrouped and set them down."

Despite that lengthy list of future major-league talent, the 1988 Cape season belonged to Dave Staton out of Orange Coast College.

Staton, a six-foot-five, two hundred and fifteen-pound first baseman playing for Brewster, hit sixteen home runs, drove in forty-six runs and hit .359, narrowly missing the triple crown because of Knoblauch's .361 batting average. His numbers, however, were good enough to chalk up league MVP honors.

According to Cape Cod league historian Bruce Hack, no modern-day player has ever won the Triple Crown. The closest anyone has come since Staton was in 1998 when another Brewster player, Bobby Kielty, missed the feat by a home run during the 1998 season.

The '88 season was special in Brewster, not only because of the success of Staton, but because it was the inaugural season for the Whitecaps. The Cape Cod league expanded from eight to ten teams that season, also adding a franchise in Bourne.

Part of the season-opening festivities in Brewster was having different professional sports personalities participate in certain events throughout the season. Appearances by Hall of Famer Stan Musial and Boston Celtics forward Kevin McHale were something that pumped up the entire team and town with maybe the exception of Staton.

"In my mind, Kevin McHale was arch-enemy number one," said Staton a life-long, die-hard Los Angeles Lakers fan.

Knoblauch and Staton battled to the very end with the batting title decided on the final day of the regular season.

"I had already ordered the Triple Crown trophy before the game started," said league president Judy Walden-Scarafile.

"It came down to the last game of the season," said Staton, who played two seasons in the big leagues with the San Diego Padres. "We played a day game and Chuck was playing at night so my stats would've been known before Chuck played. I started the game 2-for-2 and then Coach (Joe) Walsh asked me if I wanted to come out of the game. He figured Chuck would have to go something like 5-for-5 or 6-for-6 or something like that if I came out. I told him I wanted to keep playing. I didn't want to come out for that stuff."

Staton, who was inducted into the Cape Cod league Hall of Fame in 2004, admits the hitting title was on his mind heading into the game, but it wasn't the sole thought going through his head.

"I wanted to win the game," he said. "I think it was more on the minds of the manager and the GM. If it was the only thing on my mind, I would've come out of the game. If I'm going to lose a batting title, I'm glad it was to someone like Chuck Knoblauch."

Later that night, Knoblauch's Gatemen hosted the Cotuit Kettleers, who were forced to play a makeup game at Bourne earlier in the day, a game in which the Kettleers prevailed, 9-0.

Since the Kettleers had to play two that day, both games were seven-inning affairs. The shortened game, combined with a five-hit shutout from Cotuit's Mark Carper (Stanford), meant Knoblauch would only get up to the plate three times.

Knoblauch, however, recorded two of those five hits in Wareham's 5-0 loss.

Knoblauch opened his final regular-season Cape Cod league game with a liner off pitcher Carper's backside, but was eventually thrown out at first as the ball ricocheted to the third baseman, who threw to first and Wareham's speedy infielder by a split second.

"Knoblauch smoked a liner up the middle, but the ball hit Carper right in the buttocks," said John Wylde, the GM of the Wareham Gatemen and the official scorer in the game. "Knoblauch kind of hesitated in disgust after the ball hit the pitcher. The ball deflected to the third baseman, who fumbled it, and threw him out. As the official scorer, I was sweating bullets on that one.

"The next two times up, he hit line drives. They weren't hit all that well, but they weren't flares. One was to left-center and one to right-center. If my memory serves me correctly, we didn't know what Staton had done earlier that day."

Although it was Staton's ability to hit for average that made things interesting on the last day of the regular season, it was his power numbers that really made people take notice.

"In all my years there, I've never seen it where the other team just stopped what they were doing when Dave Staton was up there taking batting practice," said Walsh, now the head baseball coach at Harvard University. "I mean this guy hit moon shots. It was really like watching a major-league home-run contest before an all-star game. He had arms like Dave Winfield. He had huge feet. Trying to get spikes for him was ridiculous because he had like a size seventeen."

"It's nice to hear that people stopped and watched me hit, but I was completely oblivious and unaware of that," said Staton, who has been a California Highway Patrol officer for the last seven years. "It never crossed my mind that people were watching me. But I can tell you that when I reached the big leagues with the Padres, I know I was doing that to guys like Barry Bonds, Mark McGwire, and Mike Piazza. I'd go out there and just watch them hit.

"I remember when I first reached the big leagues, in my first trip to Houston, I watched Jeff Bagwell take BP. I went over to talk to him when he was done. I was always interested to know if those guys remembered me from the Cape like I remembered them."

Not only was Staton big, he was one of the strongest guys in the league.

"Dave Staton was like that old Sidd Finch story," said Henry Manning, the catcher on the 1988 Brewster squad. "I remember being in the outfield when I first saw him. I was watching this guy as he was launching every other pitch about 420 feet. At that point, I was thinking, 'Yeah, this guy can help us out.'"

"When he shook my hand for the first time, he pretty much crushed my hand—what a grip," said Chris Slattery, another Whitecap teammate of Staton's. Slattery, another of the twenty chosen to play in Florida, was a Division III player out of Suffolk University and hit fourth in the Brewster lineup, while Staton, the RBI machine, hit fifth.

"I probably hit even lower in the lineup when I first got there because nobody really knew who I was or the type of hitter I was," said Staton. "I usually hit anywhere from third to fifth. Wherever they wanted to put me was fine with me."

Although Staton was among the league leaders in nearly every offensive category and was a member of that all-star team which played in the Boardwalk & Baseball Tournament, his memories of the Florida trip aren't exactly pleasant.

"I was happy to be a part of the team," Staton said. "I was glad to represent Brewster, but I was somewhat frustrated because I sat the bench for most of those games. I remember riding the pine a lot and being frustrated. Making that team was never a goal of mine, but I was thrilled to be a part of that team with that group of guys."

Home runs certainly were a daily part of Staton's routine and he hit them at an alarming rate. His offensive numbers were fantasy like.

He led the league in total bases with 112. To put that number into perspective, Knoblauch finished second with 85. Staton also had a .772 slugging percentage, while Bagwell (.514) and Knoblauch (.503) were the only other players higher than .500.

"Dave Staton was the Dave Kingman of the Cape Cod league," said Bob Whalen, the manager of the Chatham Athletics in 1988 and now the head baseball man at Dartmouth College.

"At first, he would hit it out or strike out, but later on in the season he developed some real good hitting skills, and in the last month you couldn't get the guy out. He had real good plate coverage. You could throw it anywhere and he'd find a way to get the barrel of the bat on it."

"All I can say is it was a great, magical season for me," Staton said. "I got off to a quick start and that lifted my confidence. I don't remember having an extended slump that year. I started off hot and was pretty consistent."

Whalen had the unenviable task of throwing batting practice at the 1988 all-star game in Orleans. He also tossed balls for the home-run hitting contest.

"I remember telling myself just to keep my lips behind the L-screen," Whalen said. "I mean I was tight-assing it behind there because balls were just whizzing past my head. I was wondering if they would think I was a wimp if I asked for another screen."

The home-run hitting contest came down to Frank Thomas of Orleans and Staton in the semifinals of the Eastern Division in front of a packed house.

"Bo Jackson, who went to Auburn with Frank Thomas, sent Thomas some of his pro bats," Walsh said. "We used Rawlings bats, which were league bats, but they weren't quite as good as the ones Bo Jackson sent. During the home-run hitting contest, Thomas used Bo's bats. Thomas ended up winning the contest, but after it was over, Staton asked Thomas if he could take a swing with one of the bats. He hit a line drive over the center-field fence, an absolute moon shot, and Frank's jaw just dropped."

"I still think I beat him," laughed Staton. "I hit two fair they called foul."

Staton also smacked a homer in the all-star game.

"In the first inning, he hit a rope that went about ten feet off the ground over the center field fence," Slattery said.

"I knew I hit it hard and I remember it being a line drive to center," Staton said. "I didn't watch it because I was running all the way. That home run was one of my biggest highlights of the year."

"Dave Staton could hit the hell out of the ball," said Mike

Truschke, a catcher for Harwich in 1988 and 1989. "You had to be very careful with him because he really tore it up. He was just a big guy who could really hit. I guess it was just tough to find a position for him. They stuck him at first and he certainly was no J.T. Snow over there."

"He was a big, raw kid and was all bat," Wedge said of Staton. "He was a very strong guy. He stood out as a hitting prospect, but they just didn't have a place to put him."

"Staton actually came in as a third baseman," Slattery said, "but he was out of place there. He's this big guy and I think he thought he was five foot, eleven inches or something."

"I came primarily as a first baseman," Staton said. "Slattery also played first base so I told Coach Walsh I'd be willing to play third if they wanted me to. I played maybe 15 –20 games at third. I'm smart enough to know I didn't have any speed and wasn't real quick. I wanted to win and try to do what was best for our team."

"I think not having a position really hurt him in his pro career," Meek said. "I think at times he was also his own worst enemy. He had a lot of ability, a lot of power, but he didn't seem as aware or perceptive as most of the other guys. He didn't get the most of his talent. I didn't see the drive in him as I did with Eric Wedge, Bagwell, Mo, Chuck, and those other guys. I don't think he had that ingredient that made the great ones great."

What's most remarkable about Staton's performance is that he didn't play baseball the year prior to coming to the Cape because, in Staton's words, "a scholarship evaporated right before my eyes."

Ironically, after having strong high school and junior college seasons, no major league clubs came knocking on Staton's door.

"I got drafted by the Pirates right before going to the Cape," he said. "They drafted me in the year I didn't play. I couldn't figure that one out. I didn't sign with the Pirates, but I was still their property and they were very interested in me playing in the Cape Cod league."

After Staton's MVP season on the Cape, against arguably the best crop of future major-leaguers in the league's history, he assumed he would jump into pro ball.

"I was having a great season and I was thinking I was going to sign with the Pirates," he said.

The Pittsburgh organization showed even more interest when Staton and the Cape all-stars headed south for that Boardwalk & Baseball tourney.

"I went to Bradenton, where the Pirates train, when I was down in Florida and they put me through a workout," Staton said. "I thought I did an A-plus job. They told me they would be in touch with me and I went home.

"A Pirate scout came to my house and I was very excited. I was ready to go. Then he told me what they were offering me. He actually told me he didn't feel good about making the offer and he told me I should decline the $10,000 they were willing to give me. That just tore the heart out of my chest. I never did find out what the reason for the low offer was with the Pirates."

Staton then found himself in a state of limbo.

"At that point, I thought 'Holy Crud, I'm a junior, where do I go now?'" he said.

One of the schools initially interested in Staton was Northwestern, where Larry Cochell, now the head coach at Oklahoma, was coaching. Cochell spent just the 1987 season as the head coach of the Wildcats before heading to Cal State Fullerton, where Cochell offered Staton a full ride right before the semester began.

"I thought it was strange that a major college would just happen to have a full scholarship three days before school began," Staton said.

Staton had another great season in college and was a fifth-round pick of the San Diego Padres in 1989. He was called up to the big-league club in 1993 and played parts of two seasons with the Padres before his career ended in 1995 as a member of the Milwaukee Brewers Triple-A club.

"Baseball was the love of my life," said Staton, who still follows baseball religiously and lists Derek Jeter as his and his son Evan's favorite player. "It was all I wanted to do. It was hard for me to watch it in 1996 and 1997 because I felt I should've still been playing. I felt I had to move my life in another direction. I didn't want to spend ten years in Triple-A. I put my heart and soul into baseball and my career didn't last as long as I wanted it to. I'd certainly like to be one of those guys (from the 1988 Cape season) who are still playing, but I'm very happy with what I'm doing now."

CAPE COD LEAGUE

NCAA
SUMMER BASEBALL

DAVID STATON
BREWSTER WHITECAPS

The 1988 season belonged to David Staton, who narrowly missed becoming the first Cape leaguer to win the Triple Crown. The 1988 season featured many future major leaguers.

Part of the beauty of the Cape Cod league is the unknown—not knowing exactly who the players are when they first hit the field. Usually, it's years down the road, after the player cracks the majors, when the memories of having watched him play in the Cape resurface. The 1988 season is a bit different as many of those players arrived with the proverbial can't-miss label.

Mo Vaughn was certainly one of those prospects.

"When Mo Vaughn came to Wareham in 1987, I just looked at him and thought this is a man among boys," said Ace Adams, a former Cape player, a long-time assistant and the manager of the Falmouth Commodores from 1992-94. "He was playing first base and I was coaching first for Cotuit one game and there was a ground ball hit to Chuck Knoblauch. Mo stretched and the ball hit him square in the forehead. The ball went about fifty yards away and it didn't even faze him. I was thinking, 'you've got to be kidding me.'"

"Mo and I grew up playing against each other," said Truschke who went to Pepperdine, but grew up in Connecticut. "Of all the big names that year, you knew he would make it big. He was a cut above the rest. I don't know what it was, but he always seemed to tear us apart. He had his real big games against us."

Despite his size, Vaughn wasn't limited to playing first base for the Gatemen, who captured the Cape Cod league championship in 1988.

"I was at the game where Mo Vaughn caught both games of a doubleheader," said long-time scout Bill Enos.

"Mo actually didn't show that much power when he was here," Meek said. "He may have hit five homers or so, but he was a very confident guy—a real competitor. You knew that whatever his ability was, he was going to get the most out of it."

Thomas was another sure-fire player.

"Frank Thomas was a mountain of a man," Truschke said. "I only knew about him because I knew he had played football at Auburn."

"Frank Thomas was all legs," said Manning. "His legs were bigger than me. I'm six-feet and his legs alone are six-feet."

"I remember going to Orleans for the first time," said Richard Cordani, the Bourne Braves' third baseman in 1988. "I remember it well. The Lakers were in the finals and a bunch of us were hoping they'd lose. There was a guy standing over there for Orleans and we were all in awe. He was six foot, six inches, two hundred-something pounds and it was Frank Thomas. I remember saying if that guy can't make it to the big leagues, nobody can."

"Frank Thomas, like Mo Vaughn, didn't have great power numbers there either," Meek said. "He might have hit five or six, but he hit three of them against us—in one night. He put on a show that night. He hit 1,200 feet of home runs in that one game."

"Don't get me started on Frank," said Castleberry, Thomas' field manager. "With a week left in the season—and he did the same thing with the Pan Am team the year before—he had some tendinitis in his ankle, but it really didn't affect him that much. He said he wanted to go home. He had one excuse after another as to why he couldn't stay here.

"One day we were going to have a meeting in the clubhouse and he didn't see me standing there. It was pretty dark in there and he had his headphones on, he's bopping pretty good and not limping at all. He finally sees me and starts limping and saying his ankle was killing him. I told him we'd DH him. This was a week before the playoffs and we needed one win to get in so I told him once we got in, he could just pinch hit. He wouldn't even have to run. He really wanted to go home. Believe it or not, one of his excuses was that he wanted to go home and get in shape for BASEBALL. At that point, I just told him to pack his stuff and go home.

"I don't mean to pick on Frank, but he told me once that he needed to get more time at first base. We had J.T. playing there, so once in a while I'd put J.T. in left and play Frank, but he said he wanted more time at first. Here's J.T., a guy who would save about twenty runs a season defensively, and we used him in left for a few games. I told Frank that if he wanted to get better, he'd have to work at it, and I told him I'd come out with him every day and work. He never wanted to do that.

"I took a lot of heat from the people in Brewster because I pushed for Frank to make the all-star game and into the starting lineup ahead of Staton. In fact, Frank hit a triple in the game. Here's a guy who's supposed to have bad ankles."

Scott Centala, a relief pitcher out of Texas A&M, got to know Thomas pretty well during his first day on Cape Cod.

"I had committed early to play in Alaska, but the Fairbanks team I was going to folded," said Centala, who pitched for Orleans in '88. "I called my college coach and he made a few calls and I was able to get with a Cape team. I flew out there right away. Actually, I flew out there the day of the first game and got there in the fifth inning. I got my uniform in the sixth inning and I threw the eighth. At the end of the game, I didn't know what to do, where to go. I was told, 'go with this guy.' That guy was Frank Thomas and I roomed with him.

"He was a down-to-earth guy, especially with the people who were close to him. He was very confident in a close circle, but to others, he came across as arrogant. He and I worked as handymen at a place called Brewster Green—it was like a resort or some type of condominiums. We were in charge of upkeeping the grounds and stuff like that. The guy who would show us around was named Aref. I think he was from Afghanistan. He kept calling Frank 'tank'— that's just the way he pronounced it—and it sure seemed to fit."

The summer of 1988 was very special to Centala, who made it all the way to Triple-A with the Kansas City Royals, because of a milestone he reached off the baseball field.

"I turned twenty-one that summer," he said, "and I remember going up to Boston to celebrate. I remember driving Frank's car on the way there. Frank was in the front seat, J.T. Snow and a guy by the name of Jason Klonoski were in the back seat. We had a great time. I also remember hanging out at Nauset Beach on the Fourth of July with a bunch of those guys. These are the things that stick with you for life."

Centala was one of several Aggies playing in the Cape in '88, with Knoblauch being the most recognized.

"Chuck and I go way back," Centala said. "Chuck played for

Wareham and they beat us in the championship game and he would always show me his ring when I saw him."

According to Centala, Knoblauch was a big-time prospect right after high school despite not playing his senior year.

"Chuck sat out his entire senior season in high school because he broke his leg," Centala said. "He broke the weight-bearing bone and was out for the season. He still made All-American as a high school senior even though he didn't play. It was an honorary thing, but it shows you how good he was."

"Of all those guys who played that season, if there was one I had to say was the one sure guy to make it big it would be Knoblauch," said Meek. "This kid was driven. He could run and was a great hitter. He was very tough on himself."

Bagwell came to the Cape from the University of Hartford, but wasn't as recognized as Vaughn or Thomas. The power-hitting first baseman for the Houston Astros, who played for Chatham in 1987 and '88, simply dedicated himself to becoming a better player.

"The bat was swingin' him in '87," said Adams, an assistant in Chatham during Bagwell's first Cape summer. "He was a very hard worker. He wore my ass out in batting practice. You couldn't throw enough BP to that guy."

"Jeff Bagwell always, always had great hitting skills," said Whalen. "He always wanted extra work. He wanted to get better—was always showing up early. We lost our catcher at the end of the season and he told me if I needed him to go back there, he'd do it. That's something I'll never forget."

"The thing that stuck out most about Bagwell was his bat," Meek said. "Athletically, he was probably middle of the road, but he was a tough kid who made consistent contact. You could tell he had a passion for hitting."

Tim Salmon came to Cotuit from Grand Canyon College, not exactly one of the more high-profiled schools in the nation.

"I think playing on the Cape put him on the map," said Salmon's teammate Troy Buckley. "He came from a smaller school and he was able to show people he could play against some of the best talent in the country. I think he was a little overwhelmed in the beginning. I bet he struck out nine or ten of his first sixteen at-bats, but then he really heated up. He was a tremendous talent and a good, down-to-earth guy. He was a happy-go-lucky type of person who went about his work the right way."

Another big name, a future National League MVP, was a teammate of Salmon's in Cotuit but never finished the 1988 season.

"Jeff Kent played for us at Cotuit and quit," Adams said. "He was crying in the shed and he was saying we took it too seriously here. He was pampered, very immature. He was the only guy I ever hit in BP. He was a candy-ass. He wouldn't hustle and he didn't play hard. He quit pretty early, about a month into the season. Obviously, he's matured now and maybe that experience helped him a little."

"Jeff quit. He had an argument with Ace," said Arnold Mycock, the Kettleers GM at the time. "Jeff was a guy with a quick temper. He left very respectfully. He handed me his uniform and said he no longer wanted to play for (Adams).

"I remember going out there to scout him at UC-Berkley before he came here. He had a lot of power back then, too."

"You know it seems like he was only there a week or so," said Salmon of Kent. "I hardly got to know him then. He was very talented and I got the impression he took it seriously. He was very confident on and off the field and didn't seem to mix with the team much. I figured it was a focus more on his part not to let anything get in the way.

"I think the league was a good training ground for advancing in the game. It was serious because people on the East Coast take their baseball seriously. It was serious because it is the most talented league and most scouted. You bring in good players and it will become more serious because that's what it takes to be successful against the best. It was just a tough league, and I think all the players are stretched and tested a little more than they're used to. But that is good if you want to go on."

Buckley, a catcher/first baseman out of Santa Clara University vaguely remembers Kent's disappearing act.

"I do remember there was some confrontation with the coach," Buckley said, "and that was the last we saw of him. Jeff and I went on a recruiting trip together to Cal. He pretty much kept to himself, did his own thing. I got to the park one day and he wasn't there. I heard he went home."

Staton has his own Kent story.

"One thing that stands out about Jeff Kent up there was in a game at Brewster where he struck out maybe two or three times," he said. "He had a little bit of a temper. After he struck out, he made his way behind the dugout. Nobody could really see him, but I was at first base so I was able to see what was going on and he was so mad, he tried to break the bat over his knee. Only the bat didn't break and he wound up hobbling around."

Buckley, a ninth-round draft pick of the Minnesota Twins in 1989, said he agrees the Cape Cod league takes summer baseball seriously, but doesn't necessarily look at that as a negative.

"They want to win," he said. "In college, there's a lot of emphasis on winning. Some guys, when they come to play summer ball, they're trying to work on things to improve. I guess it all depends on the individual. Coach (Pete) Varney and Ace ran a tight ship. They were serious about winning and there's nothing wrong with that, but some people will think it's too serious.

"The one thing I noticed about the Cape was, in my opinion, it was tough to build cohesiveness as a team. There were a lot of individuals in the league, worried about stats and that sort of thing."

Buckley was another member of the Kettleers who didn't last a full season, but it wasn't because he was unhappy. He left late in the summer because a knee injury he suffered during his sophomore season at Santa Clara required some rehabbing.

"I struggled immensely," said Buckley, now an assistant baseball coach at Long Beach State. "I came here as a catcher and I just had no flexibility. I caught maybe once or twice when I was in Cotuit. I was mainly there as a bat. When you're asked to just hit and you're not hitting well, it can be real tough. For me, I was struggling, I was away from home for the first time and I was failing for the first time. It was tough.

"As much as I struggled there, I had a great time there. I have a lot of respect for the league. I valued the fact they respected me enough to play there. The league is run by a bunch of volunteers who have a passion for the game and it shows.

"Some of the things I remember most are playing in the tough parks. I remember all the fog in Chatham. And I remember the announcer in Orleans, who would be talking during your at-bats, while the guy was throwing a pitch. My time up there was a great experience and it was the best thing to prepare me for pro ball."

This is a team photo of the 1988 champion Wareham Gatemen. Chuck Knoblauch is in the middle row, third from the left. Mo Vaughn is in the middle row, second from the right.

Chapter 5
Off the Field

"For me, there was definitely some culture shock. I had never lived outside Texas before. I was used to it being 100 degrees every day. I remember wearing sleeves on July 28 when it was about 80 outside and everyone was saying how hot it was."
–Lance Berkman, Wareham '96

"One year, my job was a night watchman at a marina in Harwichport. That really is one of the dumbest jobs to give a player because you have to go in at midnight after leaving the ballpark at about 11 or so. Well, one night, I fell asleep on the job and someone stole a boat. Luckily, they found it the next day without any damage, but needless to say I had another job a few days later—working at Bradlees."
–John Schiffner, known as the 'Cape Cod God' after spending thirty years in the Cape Cod league as a player and field manager.

Not only are Cape Cod Baseball League players learning to adjust to using wooden bats, throwing inside, and playing against the elite collegiate talent throughout the country, several of them also wind up modifying their everyday lifestyle when they come to play baseball in New England. A few struggle with being away from home. Some find it a bit awkward getting used to living with host families. Others have a tough time balancing their work schedule with their baseball schedule. And there are those who simply have a difficult time getting used to the northeastern cuisine.

"I remember it was pretty much my first time being up north and I didn't know what steamers (steamed clams) were," said Deric Ladnier, the Kansas City Royals director of scouting, who played for Falmouth in 1984.

"I remember trying them and having a ton of sand in my mouth." Mike Rouse, an infielder from the West Coast who attended Cal

State Fullerton, came to Massachusetts in 2000 and was a key member of the league champion Brewster Whitecaps. A fifth-round draft pick of the Blue Jays in 2001 and now a member of the Oakland Athletics' Triple-A affiliation Sacramento River Cats, Rouse said it didn't take long for him to get used to that famous New England seafood.

"My most memorable moment was definitely winning the championship there," said Rouse. "But one of the best parts was eating all that seafood, man. I think I had fried shrimp every night."

"I remember ordering an iced tea," said Houston Astros outfielder Lance Berkman, "and being from Texas, I'm used to getting this big jug with a whole lot of ice, but up there they give you a little glass with little ice."

The glass of iced tea was only one of the few instances which made Berkman realize he wasn't deep in the heart of Texas anymore.

"For me, there was definitely some culture shock," he said. "I had never lived outside Texas before. I was used to it being 100 degrees every day. I remember wearing sleeves on July 28 when it was about 80 outside and everyone was saying how hot it was."

Brad Cresse, a catcher for the Tucson Sidewinders, the Arizona Diamondbacks Triple-A affiliate, played for Chatham in 1997, and although most of his Cape Cod memories are baseball related, there's another one that stands out.

"I remember the parks the most about the league," Cresse said. "In Hyannis, we had to play day games all the time because there was a bird's nest up in the lights. In Bourne, the sun would set in center field and we'd have to have sun delays. In Chatham, we even had a few fog-outs.

"But one thing that really stands out was when my host dad came up to me one day and said he was going to go PAAHHK THE CAAAHH. I just looked at him and said, 'What?' It was definitely the first time I had ever heard that."

The Cape Cod league does more than prepare college players for the next baseball level. It also strives to give these young college students an opportunity to experience life outside of baseball. In short, it gives them a taste of the real world. Players are required to pay rent to their host families, and in order to secure the finances to make the payment, the league sets the players up with daytime jobs, ranging anywhere from running baseball clinics to making pizzas.

"Working is voluntary, but we like them to have jobs," said Hester Grue, president of the Brewster Whitecaps. "It gets them up and going, and also tends to dissuade them from partying too much. We also want them to interact with the community because kids really do look up to them. I always tell them, they represent the team and they represent the league."

Some of the jobs can be challenging, others not quite so demanding.

"I worked on a golf course," said Jason Grove, an outfielder in the New York Yankees farm system, who played for Wareham in 1999. "I replaced divots."

Scott Williamson (Chatham '96), a middle reliever with the Boston Red Sox, also worked at a golf course, with the word 'worked' used loosely—very loosely.

"He had to be the laziest kid ever," laughed Charlie Thoms, the GM of the Chatham Athletics and Williamson's host parent that season. "He was supposed to be a groundskeeper at Eastward Ho Country Club. I drove him there the first day—it was about two miles away. Two hours later, here he is WALKING back, saying 'you should've seen what they wanted us to do.' He lasted one day."

He wasn't the only one with a short-lived job.

"At first, Dan Reichert and I worked at a grocery store," said Rich Thieme, a pitcher out of Georgia Tech who played for Bourne in 1996. "It was not for us. We quit after a week.

"Then we worked for the Bourne Department of Education cutting grass. Dan was a little too slow to the punch and I got to ride the lawn mower all summer. He had to weed-eat. It was a pretty fun job, and we became very familiar with Dunkin' Donuts."

Chatham Hardware has been a staple in the Cape Cod league for more than thirty-five years, providing Cape Cod league players with an opportunity to make some cash while learning how to deal with the public in a working environment. Chatham Hardware was where Thurman Munson worked when he hit .420 for Chatham in 1967.

George Tamer, the fourth owner of Chatham Hardware in its sixty-three-year history, is always looking to take in a ballplayer from the Cape Cod league—under one condition.

"We don't want any prima donnas," said Tamer. "What we try to do is put them on as a normal employee. They will do everything that has to be done. They will work the register, stock shelves, they'll even sweep the floor. One of our goals is to make it so they experience a normal working environment.

"It's not just a job here. We hope they get a positive experience out of it. We hope to have them work on their people skills and their business skills."

Others, like Cresse, bypass the opportunity to work and devote the majority of their time to baseball.

"I didn't have a job there," said Cresse. "My dad told me if I dedicated myself and if I lifted weights, he'd take care of me. I lifted at Willy's Gym in Orleans every day."

J.C. Holt, who came to the Cape out of Louisiana State University and won the Cape Cod league batting title by hitting .388 for Brewster in 2003, was another player who bypassed summer employment.

"I woke up at eight and went to the gym," Holt said. "I went for about an hour and a half. I'd also go and hit early. I just didn't want to be distracted. I did do some camps when I was there and got paid for that, but that wasn't very often."

"Some guys come in here and they're in an intense weightlifting regimen and they don't want to disturb that," Thoms said. "In some cases, you can't blame them. If they're going to be a top draft pick, you can see why they would just dedicate their time to baseball."

Berkman said he was grateful to be given one of the more laid-back jobs because some of the work can have an effect on players' performances on the baseball diamond.

"I think it's great that you're given a job," Berkman said. "It was better for my family for me to pay my way through playing there. Some guys have tougher jobs, doing yard maintenance all day, and that's probably not beneficial to them, but I had a decent job. It teaches responsibility and that's good because college is all about growing up."

Chris Sabo, a third baseman who played a major part in Cincinnati's 1990 World Series victory over the Oakland Athletics, got paid for being a clubhouse attendant. He was in charge of cleaning the uniforms when he was with Orleans in 1982. Former Cleveland Indians slugger Cory Snyder delivered groceries to restaurants. John Franco worked at a car wash. Robin Ventura worked at Puritan Clothing Company in Hyannis, doing "all the little things they asked me to do."

Tim Salmon was employed by E.E.C. Swift Co., a local market in Osterville, but don't ask him how to get there.

"I couldn't tell you exactly where it was because I never drove there," said Salmon. "I didn't have a car so I never really paid much attention to directions. My roommate, Brian Shabosky from Wake Forest, drove me everywhere.

"Working at Swift's really was great. The manager was an older man named Howard Bearse. He really took good care of me. I was given a lot of responsibility, which really helped the time to pass. Swift's was a stop on the way to the beach for most so it was always busy. My duties were working the register, making sandwiches in the deli, stocking, and bagging ice. It really was a fun job and that's because of Howie and the others I worked with."

Berkman had quite an unusual occupation.

"I was assistant to the mayor (actually the town administrator)," Berkman said. "One of the things we did was go out and do house surveys. Me and a teammate, Jeff Andra, were given a map of Wareham and we basically went out and rated the condition of the houses. One guy would go out and drive and the other would write down the notes."

Although the risk of getting injured while working a Cape Cod league job is virtually non-existent, it can happen—even while employed as a painter.

"Eric Wedge, the current manager of the Cleveland Indians, was one of my favorite players," said Don Reed, who skippered Yarmouth-Dennis, Wareham and was an assistant coach in Chatham during a healthy CCBL managerial career that spanned two decades.

"He was working for a painter. I remember him telling me his shoulder was hurting and I kept asking him if there was a play where he remembered getting hit or if he hurt it swinging the bat, but he said no. He played hurt and was just tough as nails. Come to find out, he was rolling ceilings during his job and that's how he hurt himself. Needless to say, we sure as heck got that taken care of."

"I remember I worked for the president of the team, Dick Thomas," said Wedge. "He was a handy-man type of guy. I did a lot of odd jobs, and painting was one of them. I do remember having some soreness in my shoulder. I don't know for sure if painting was what caused it, but it was an unnatural motion and that may have had something to do with it."

Anaheim Angels outfielder Darin Erstad, playing for Falmouth in the early '90s, had just as successful a stint with his employment as he did on the baseball diamond.

"Darin came here as a freshman," said Falmouth Commodores GM Chuck Sturtevant, who developed such a strong bond with the center fielder, he was invited to Erstad's wedding. "He worked at Bradlees (department store) and he was the employee of the month. He had the record for most sales. That's just the type of person he is."

"I worked with Darin at Bradlees as a cashier," said Don Nestor, an all-star pitcher with the Commodores in 1993. "We were both cashiers. He was named employee of the month and I was pissed. Darin was a stud. He was built like Adonis, could run like the wind, and now he winds up as employee of the month? It was amazing. He had everything going for him. I do have to admit, though, he was a great cashier."

Jason Garman, a teammate of Nestor and Erstad in 1993, spent his summer mornings working at Stop & Shop. An all-star pitcher out of Princeton, Garman even got an interesting perk out of bagging groceries at the supermarket.

"When I was working there, I met this woman and her family," Garman recalled. "She had a son with cerebral palsy. She asked me if I was a baseball player. I told her I was and we eventually became pretty friendly. Her husband was an entertainment lawyer in New York and Stephen King was one of his clients. One night I got to go up to Fenway with Stephen King and watch a game."

Scott Mudd (Indiana) and Tim Kraus (Notre Dame) were also players on the 1993 Falmouth squad who held jobs at Bradlees. According to Nestor, they weren't as serious on the job as they were when it came to playing ball.

"I remember one day I went on break and they came out and they were just sopping wet," Nestor said. "I was thinking, 'man these guys are working way too hard.' Come to find out, they had two hockey nets set up in the back room and were playing hockey the whole time."

While many of the players excelled at their summer jobs, others weren't quite as good.

John Schiffner, who came to the Cape as a player in 1974 and played in parts of three seasons, wasn't quite as successful on the job as Erstad.

"One year, my job was a night watchman at a marina in Harwichport," said Schiffner, who has been the manager for the Chatham Athletics for the past ten seasons and is referred to as the "Cape Cod God."

"That really is one of the dumbest jobs to give a player because you have to go in at midnight after leaving the ballpark at about eleven or so. Well, one night, I fell asleep on the job and someone stole a boat. Luckily, they found it the next day without any damage, but needless to say I had another job a few days later—working at Bradlees.

Another year, Schiffner had a job as a lifeguard, which also nearly got him into some trouble.

"My roommate was also a lifeguard and one day he tells me to come by his beach and check out this girl," Schiffner recalled. "He tells me there's a gorgeous blonde who's always there and she's just stunning. I was off one day so I went there and I started talking to her. She was from Texas. After being there a little while, I told her I had to get going because I had a game that night. She asked if she could come to the game.

"She shows up at the game and you can hear the buzz when she was there. She really was drop-dead gorgeous. Word got out that she was there to see me. Bob Stead, who just resigned as the Cape Cod league's commissioner, was coaching third for Y-D that season and I was playing third for Harwich and he asked me if she was here to see me. I said, 'kinda.'

"Later in the game I hit a home run and she got a hold of a ball. I don't know if it was THE ball, but after the game she asked me to sign it. After the games, we'd usually go out for a few drinks—the drinking age was eighteen back then—so I asked her if she wanted to join us for a drink. She was hesitant, but I said, 'come on.'

"On the way there, she tells me she won't be able to get into the bar. She said she wasn't old enough. I told her not to worry because she looked twenty. Then I got curious and asked her how old she was—seventeen?, sixteen? She said thirteen. I hit the brakes real hard and stopped the car.

"I didn't want to completely ruin her night, so I took her to Dairy Queen. I then went home and I was desperately trying to avoid seeing my roommate because I didn't want to have to explain anything to him. Of course, he was sitting there, and he asked me how it went and why I was back so early. I just said she couldn't get in. He asked why. I told him she was thirteen. He said, 'What??' The next day at the game there were fifteen baby diapers hanging in the dugout."

Having a few beers and hanging out with the females wasn't all that uncommon a mixture. Just ask Thieme and Reichert.

"I remember when Dan Riechert and myself were hanging out with some girls after taking a long drive to the beach late one night," Thieme said. "It seemed like we drove forever and then we came to the beach. Dan, being from California, and myself, from Atlanta, we had our ideas of beaches, but this one was so different. It was very foggy and a little chilly. We got out of the car and walked out on the beach and saw a lot of rocks out in the ocean. We joked that we might have stumbled upon Plymouth Rock or something. We just did what many twenty-one-year-old guys with a couple of girls would do. We finished drinking our beers and tried to see where we could get with girls. The night was not good to us. We struck out and ended up with a hangover."

Sometimes the girls even got in the way.

"When Larry Bigbie was here," said Wareham president/GM John Wylde, "he was tearing it up for the first third of the season. It looked like he was going to win the batting title without any problems. I mean he was ripping extra-base hits, really driving the ball during that stretch. Then his girlfriend came. She stayed, and his average went absolutely south. He fell from about .360 or so to about .220. It got to the point where Don Reed wasn't playing him.

"Larry had a job, came for BP, played a game at night and then was spending time with his girlfriend. He was tired and he wound up seeing the light and sent her home. When she left, the original Larry Bigbie came back."

Girls, drinking, and baseball was also the recipe for a far-fetched movie based on the Cape Cod league, which was introduced to theaters in 2001. *Summer Catch*, starring Freddie Prinze and Jessica Biel, focuses on many off-the-field events on the Cape, portraying the players doing a lot of their scoring off the baseball diamond. While players in some cases do develop relationships off the field, their primary focus is playing baseball. "Summer Catch" mixes the two, but takes the non-baseball parts a little bit too far.

"The baseball part of the movie is pretty good, but the love story part is too Hollywood," said Peter Troy, the president of the Chatham A's.

The Chatham A's were the featured team in the movie, and the Troy family played a role in helping bring the movie to life.

"My family was very involved with *Summer Catch*," said Troy, "The screenwriter spent two weeks with us. That summer we had two players staying with us—Randy Flores, a left-handed pitcher, and Ryan Stromsborg a second baseman out of USC. The main character in the movie is named Ryan and is a mix of the two guys who lived with us.

"Sam Weisman, a Hollywood director, came up with the concept of using the Chatham A's. He has a house here, and he asked for my help.

"I think the funniest story about that movie happened in the summer of '96. The movie was supposed to feature two up-and-coming actors. They were a week away from filming and Fox pulled the plug. A studio executive didn't think the two kids could carry the movie. Those two kids were Ben Affleck and Matt Damon. I think they made a mistake there."

Imagine it's the single biggest day of your baseball life, something you've been anxiously awaiting for quite some time. You've been selected to play in the Cape Cod Baseball League All-Star Game and you wake up in the morning ready to play ball with the best of the best college players in the country. The game is the final piece of a daylong list of events, including an autograph session, home run hitting contest, a luncheon and much more. It may be the most significant game you've ever played, one that will be viewed by thousands of fans and, more importantly, loads of scouts. Imagine if your dream is nearly shattered because you spent the better part of the morning down at the police station, wondering if you'd ever see the playing field that day.

In 1993, Falmouth had four players selected to play in the annual all-star affair. Darin Erstad, Don Nestor, Mike Martin, and Jason Garman arrived at Fuller Field in Falmouth ready for their big day, and the only significant question at that particular moment was who was going to drive to Wareham's Spillane Field since they all had their own car in the parking lot.

"We met at the park at 9:30 and we're all looking at each other to see who's going to drive," said Martin, a second baseman out of Boston College. "I took it upon myself to say I would drive. The four of us got in and we headed to the game."

They barely made it out of the parking lot when the sounds of sirens and the glare of flashing lights caught Martin's eye and he pulled aside to let the approaching police car pass by.

"The police pulled me over," Martin said. "I had no idea what was going on. Come to find out, they told me I had an expired inspection sticker. The cop goes back to his car and I'm thinking it's not really that big of a deal. Instead, he comes back and tells me to get out of the car. He tells me my license is suspended and asks me if I knew it. I told him I didn't know that and he said it was because of an unpaid speeding ticket from a few years ago. It wound up being from a ticket

I had contested years back and had never heard anything about it. "Then he searches the car. I think he was a Falmouth Rent-a-Cop or something. He finds baseball bats in the back and tells me they can be used as weapons. It was unbelievable. They impound the car, they cuff me, and they book me."

"When the cop said we couldn't take the car, we couldn't figure out how the heck we were going to get to Wareham," Garman said. "Mike came back to the car with a look on his face like he couldn't believe what was going on. He said, 'I think they're going to arrest me.'"

"It seemed so ridiculous when we got pulled over," Nestor said. "I didn't know what the heck to do. It was quite the experience."

For nearly two hours, the Falmouth Foursome were at the police station and Martin was secluded in his tiny holding cell.

"The guys were watching me through a camera as I was pacing in my little cell on probably the biggest day of my life," Martin said. "I'm sure they could've gone and tried to find a way to get to the game, but Darin wouldn't leave. He said to the other guys, 'we're staying with him.' He held them together and wouldn't let me go through that alone."

Just about lunchtime, Martin was released and the players were able to make it safely to Wareham. They missed the autograph session and a few of the early-morning festivities, but were able to take part in the big game.

When they arrived at the field, they were greeted by the other players, and one upset Commodore coach.

"I was pissed," said Falmouth field manager Ace Adams. "I had no idea what was going on. Here I was at the all-star game and none of my players showed up."

Martin said when the four showed up for the game, rumors were flying about what had happened and people had a tough time believing what actually took place.

"We got there and someone had started the rumor that we all had been out drinking the night before and got into a fight at a bar," Martin said. "Nothing could be further from the truth. I have no idea how that one started."

The hours spent at the police station weren't the only quality time the Falmouth Foursome had together. Since money was tight, the group was forced to cut corners when necessary, which was nearly all the time.

"I think I made seventy-five bucks a week working at Bradlees," Nestor said. "And fifty of that went to pay my rent. I remember when we went to Martha's Vineyard for the day. We hardly had any money. We hitchhiked all over the island just to get around."

Even when on the ballfield, Nestor found a way to scrape up a few extra bucks.

"Mike and Jason were the instigators on our team," he said. "They would say you ought to do this and that, and I'd do it.

"I was the closer on the team and I was having a pretty good season. I was close to breaking the save record, and toward the end of the season I was a little bit ticked because we were in a save situation and the coach didn't put me in. So the next game, we're winning something like 11-0 and he puts me in the game and I'm very upset I'm in this game and not the other one. I can't remember exactly who it was but either Mike or Jason tells me to throw one to the backstop during warm-ups—just let one fly. I said, 'ok I'll do that.' There was some money exchanged—I think it was five bucks or something.

"So I throw one way up there. I think I almost hit the press box. I immediately kicked the dirt and acted as if I slipped. Everyone on the team is rolling. Then I hear over the loudspeaker, 'hey, what did we do wrong up here?'

"I was pitching well in the inning and I remember thinking to myself that I bet I could get twenty bucks if I do that during the game. It was a nothing game. We were way ahead, so I let another one go about eight-to-ten feet up the backstop. At the end of the inning, Ace stops me and asked me if I did it on purpose. I told him I slipped. I said, 'you saw me during warm-ups.' I went back to the bench and the guys were just rolling, but I never got the twenty bucks."

"It could've been me who told him to throw it to the backstop," said Garman, "but that sounds a little more like Mike."

Coach Adams and Nestor didn't quite see eye to eye. It wasn't only because the player was roughly a foot taller than the skipper; it was because Adams was serious when it came to baseball and Nestor could've been classified as the team clown.

"He was a knucklehead," said Adams. "The kid could pitch, though."

"Ace didn't seem to like me from the beginning," Nestor said. "My college coach at South Florida, Eddie Cardieri, who had also coached in the Cape, once said to me, 'what are you doing up there? Ace hates you. He loves you on the field, though.' I don't know why. I was a good kid.

"I really am a good guy, but for whatever reason, I had a bad reputation up there. I twisted my ankle one day falling off the steps of my host family's porch. I got it treated, but I couldn't play that night. The rumor was that I did it while drinking, but that was not the case at all."

The rocky relationship between player and coach may have been ignited during their first team meeting.

"The first night we got there, we had an introduction to the community," Nestor said. "There were about seven of us shooting the shit and we hit it off real well. Darin was telling us about a dyslexic kid from Nebraska named Kurt. He said they called him Truck.

"So Ace is introducing the players and he's raving about this Notre Dame kid, who's supposed to be this great pitcher. At the time, Ace was coaching at Michigan and he was saying how upset he was because he couldn't get this kid to come to Michigan. He said this guy caused him a lot of 'nightless sleeps.' Right after he said that, I yelled, 'oh, my God, it's Truck.' Everyone there laughed. Maybe that got me off on the wrong foot with him."

The Falmouth club that season had it all—four all-stars, an outfielder (Erstad) who would go on to become the No. 1 draft pick in the country, and a top-notch closer. The talent level even went beyond the playing field as the Commodores also had a player on that team who even sang the national anthem before a game.

"Brian Cummings was a character," Nestor said. "He also worked with us at Bradlees. He was an incredibly talented singer. On July

Fourth, a bunch of us were at Falmouth Beach watching the fireworks and out of the blue he gets up and starts singing Billy Joel's 'Scenes from an Italian Restaurant.' He was great. I mean people started to gather, he was that good. Then he belted that song Ferris Bueller was singing, 'Danke Schoen,' and he was good. Then he started to lose it a little bit. He pulled his hat all the way down, pulled his pants all the way up and started calling himself Joey. I don't know why. I have no clue what the heck he was doing. He started walking up to people and just yelling, 'steak,' 'steak.' The cops come in and stop him but he stays in character. He was still acting like Joey. The cops ended up letting him go. I think they thought he was lost or something.

"We had a lot of fun together. If we could ever get the whole team together again, it would be an absolute riot. It's a situation where you wish you had a camcorder over your shoulder the entire time. It was a blast."

The traffic incident involving the Falmouth Foursome wasn't the only vehicle incident the Cape Cod league has endured.

On July 5, 2001 a simple traffic accident involving a Cotuit Kettleer player made national headlines as Jonathan Swearinger's pickup truck hit Eunice Kennedy Shriver's Jeep Cherokee. Shriver, the sister of John F. Kennedy and mother-in-law of Arnold Schwarzenegger, broke her leg in the accident, but Swearinger, who was not injured, took a lot of heat and was hounded by the media at his games.

"We had lots of newspapers, media at our games just because of that accident," Kettleers GM Bruce Murphy said.

"It was crazy. We had to have the player leave in the seventh inning and put a different jersey on so he wouldn't get bombarded by the media."

Another vehicular incident took place in 1980 when Glenn Davis was playing for the Chatham A's. Teammate Peyton Mosher let Davis have use of his car one evening and Mosher was very lucky to get it back.

"When I was an assistant coach in Chatham one year, Glenn Davis came to Chatham with a college teammate, Peyton Mosher," said Schiffner. "Peyton drove up from Georgia in his jeep and that was their vehicle to get around in. Somehow, something happened where Peyton went away for a day or two and he allowed Glenn to have the keys. That night, Glenn took a few people down to a beach and apparently he went too far down and the tide came in and the jeep got stuck. It got stuck for a while. The next day, Peyton was asking where his jeep was, and I remember Glenn running away from him. If Peyton could have killed him, he would have."

"Wow, I actually had forgotten about Glenn sinking my jeep," recalled Mosher in the fall of 2003. "Actually, he didn't sink it, he just ran it through some very large and deep puddles on the beach. It's what we in the south call puddle jumpin'. Somehow, water got caught up in the distributor cap, and the jeep started misfiring and just plain quit. We had to dry out the cap, replace the wires—all while the tide was coming in.

"We finally got the cap dry enough—you can never get all the water out. We got the engine started and limped our way out of there, backfiring all the way just before the water got to us."

The Falmouth players were unable to sign the photo because they were at the police station, supporting Mike Martin (third from left in back row), who was caught driving with a suspended license.

Practical jokes were also pretty common and were a big part of easing the tension on and off the ballfield. One prank has even remained unsolved (at least from the prankee's standpoint) for more than ten years.

"When I was coaching at Orleans, I had two assistants, Ted Lekas and Donnie Reynolds," said John Castleberry, who managed the Cardinals from 1984-1990. "They were so different. Donnie, who is the brother of Harold Reynolds, was very laid back, a fun-loving guy. Ted was a little uptight. Coaching here was very exciting for him. He brought in something like four brand-new pairs of Nikes and boy was he ready to go.

"I remember I was throwing batting practice and my wife Kate was standing next to Donnie. Ted comes over and Kate says to Ted, "what's on your shoes?" He wipes his feet and it just keeps coming. 'Shaving cream,' he yells, and then he starts pointing fingers. 'You did it,' he said to Donnie. 'You did it,' he yells at me. Donnie and I are looking at each other. After BP, Ted goes back to the clubhouse and slams the door. I asked Donnie if he did it and he said no and he asked me and I told him I thought it was a great idea, but I didn't do it. I remember whoever did it, got all his shoes.

"Before the game, I realized I had forgotten my pen and headed back to the office. When I got there, I saw one of my players down on one knee with the shaving cream. I have no idea how he got in there because the door was locked. When he looked at me, it was like a kid getting caught with his hand in the cookie jar. I looked at him and said, 'I didn't see anything,' and then I got my pen and went back to the field. To this day, Ted doesn't know who it is. He's actually said his name before when he was running down his list of suspects. He thinks he knows, but he doesn't."

Castleberry admits he was one to joke around with his players and coaches, and some of them took him seriously.

Dave Otto was a highly touted, six-foot-eight pitcher who pitched two seasons for Orleans in the early '80s and was a second-round pick of the Oakland Athletics in 1985. He pitched eight seasons in the majors.

"Dave Otto had a real bad year his first year on the Cape," said Castleberry, who was an assistant in Otto's first season. "He was something like 0-6. He was knocked out of the first inning in two different games. He really struggled. I told him when I got the head job, I wanted him to come back and he told me he wanted to come back and prove he was a much better pitcher than he showed.

"I told him I had one request for him. I'm 5-6, 5-7 and he's 6-8 so I told him whenever I go out to the mound, he has to stand off the mound so he doesn't make me look bad. One game, I go out to get the ball from him and I get to the mound and he goes over to the edge of the dirt. Here he is standing down there and leaves me standing on the mound by myself."

One of Castleberry's all-time favorite players was J.T. Snow, who came to Orleans in 1988. Maybe Castleberry was close to Snow because he was a pure hitter and a strong defensive player, or maybe it was because Snow's father Jack was a wide receiver for the Los Angeles Rams.

"I was a Rams fan," Castleberry said. "I didn't realize how good J.T. was, but I kiddingly told him that if he wanted to play for me, I needed his dad's autograph. I told him if he didn't have it when he got here, he wasn't playing. When he arrived, I extended my arm to shake his hand and he put his father's autograph in my hand. I thanked him and told him he just got himself some playing time."

Chapter 6

The Coaches

"I often tell people that coaching in the Cape Cod league is the closest thing to heaven I've ever been to."
–Rolando Casanova, Cape Cod league field manager (1989-1996)

"The one thing I'm going to regret the rest of my life was resigning after the 2000 season. I took an athletic director's job and it didn't work out for me and it's very disturbing to me. I'm working on a few important things in my life. I'm working on my doctorate right now, but if I could pick one thing to do every year for the rest of my life, it would be coaching in the Cape Cod Baseball League. I would drop my doctorate to coach up there again. I'd go as an assistant. It was that good of an experience for me."
–Mike Roberts, Cape Cod league field manager (1984, 2000, 2004)

While the players are the ones who must learn to make the biggest adjustments to baseball on the Cape, the field managers are also forced to do a little tweaking of their own. They have the unenviable task of trying to get twenty-plus players from different parts of the country to come together and work collectively toward that goal of winning a championship.

"I remember one day Don Reed (Wareham field manager) and I were at the field in the beginning of the summer and a huge U-Haul truck pulled up, a ramp comes down and three guys come out with motorcycles, headbands and said, 'I'm looking for Coach Reed,'" said Joe Walsh, Reed's pitching coach during the mid-90s. "Don and I just looked at each other and shook our heads. You just never knew what you were going to get."

Like the players, the Cape Cod league's skippers can also go on to make a name of their own. In fact, several of the league's top field managers have branched out into different sports and have become high-profiled, front-office figures. Lou Lamoriello, who coached three different teams in the Cape league and played for Orleans, has gone on to become the highly successful general manager of the New Jersey Devils. Dave Gavitt also managed in the league before becoming the Commissioner of the Big East Conference and the Chief Executive Officer of the Boston Celtics. Bill Livesey, who ranks fifth all time for wins by a Cape Cod league manager with 240, is a special assistant to the GM for the New York Mets.

Other former Cape Cod league field managers, like George Greer, who led the charge in Cotuit for nine seasons, have continued to march along the baseball patch with their coaching careers. Greer has remained one of the most respected, and successful, coaches in baseball. The former head baseball man at Wake Forest, Greer has recorded 700-plus wins as a head coach at the Division-1 college level. Walsh has also taken to the Division-1 college ranks as he is the head baseball man at Harvard, while Bob Whalen, who was the field manager for Chatham in the late '80s, is the head coach at Dartmouth College.

Some other previous CCBL field managers also have decided to remain is baseball, making their living as professional scouts.

Rolando Casanova and John Castleberry both coached in the CCBL in the '80s and early '90s and have extended their baseball lives in the world of pro baseball. Casanova is a scout for the Detroit Tigers and Castleberry is in a similar position with the Texas Rangers. Stan Meek, who managed the Wareham Gatemen in 1988, is the scouting director for the 2003 World Champion Florida Marlins.

While on the Cape, Castleberry and Meek met each other for the league title in 1988, with Meek's Gatemen winning the best-of-three series 2-1.

"I have a lot of fond memories of the Cape," said Castleberry, "and one of those was coaching against Stan for the championship. In one of those games, there was a close play at second base and the umpire at second called the guy safe and the umpire at first called him out. Immediately, Stan and I came rushing out to argue. I went to one umpire and he went to the other. People in the stands were just rolling. Apparently, we almost collided with each other and we didn't even know it."

Castleberry admits it's the playoff semifinal series against Y-D, which preceded the championship round that season, which sticks out as the best baseball he's been involved with.

"Those were the three greatest games I've ever coached," he said. "They were best I've ever seen. (Relief pitcher) Scott Centala said he didn't have a lot left in the tank, but he said he would throw if I needed him. In the bottom of the ninth, someone hit a missile right at him and he snared it. It seemed like Marty Durkin, who was playing left field, did about ten 360s out there for grabs, and a guy by the name of (Doug) Shields jumped over the fence, not once, but twice for catches for them."

Casanova, who managed the Brewster and Orleans franchises, says managing in the Cape Cod league was like a dream come true.

"I often tell people that coaching in the Cape Cod league is the closest thing to heaven I've ever been to," Casanova said. "If the weather was good, it was an absolutely beautiful place. I have some great memories, but it's funny because I don't miss it. Sounds strange, but I guess it's because I gave my heart and soul while I was up there and I was almost burned out by it. That's just the way I am.

"I interviewed at Brewster, applied in 1989, went up there and got the job. I had heard it was the elite summer league. I was at Brewster for three years, left and had no intention of going back. John Castleberry called me and asked me if I was interested in coming back. I said no. He said, 'you don't understand. I mean to come back and be the field manager for the Orleans team.' I thought that was the elite franchise and took the job in 1991."

While in Orleans, Casanova managed future big-league stars such as Nomar Garciaparra, Todd Helton, Aaron Boone and Jay Payton.

Castleberry managed in the Cape from 1982-1991 and one of the players he managed in Orleans in 1986 was Florida Marlins outfielder Jeff Conine, who was a pitcher for the Cape Cod league champion Cardinals.

"He threw a knuckleball," Castleberry said. "Early in batting practice, the pitchers would go up there and take their hacks. My assistant, Tom Yankus, would throw early BP and he said, 'boy, that Conine can really hit.'

"As a pitcher, he probably topped off at 84. He'd short-arm everything. We had a very good bullpen that year and I'd just tell him to get me through the fifth inning."

Castleberry, in addition to coaching future high-profiled players such as Frank Thomas and J.T Snow, also managed one of the most highly anticipated players ever to put on a Cape Cod league uniform.

In 1989, the Cardinals were struggling and it was becoming evident they weren't going to make the playoffs. One of Castleberry's players, Mark LaRosa, came from LSU and mentioned they might want to try and get his college teammate, Ben McDonald, to come and pitch on the Cape. McDonald had just been selected as the top pick in the nation by the Baltimore Orioles, but was stuck in negotiations and hadn't yet signed with the big-league club.

Ben McDonald (#34) pitched in one game for the Orleans Cardinals before signing with the Baltimore Orioles as the No. 1 draft pick in the majors.

"In 1989 I was coaching at George Washington and we had just gone to the regionals," Castleberry said. "I have to admit because of that, I didn't do a great job with my backup list for the Cape Cod league. Record-wise this was our worst year in Orleans and we weren't going anywhere so I thought it might be a good idea to get him here. I thought it would be a nice draw."

And a nice draw it was. Nearly five thousand fans flocked to Eldredge Park in Orleans to watch the Cardinals host the Harwich Mariners in anticipation of watching the nation's No. 1 draft pick take the mound.

"It was amazing," said Castleberry. "People drove here from all over the place. He was like a rock star. I had never seen anything like it."

McDonald took the mound for the first – and only – time in a Cape Cod league uniform, tossed a few innings and left early the following morning to go home and sign with the Orioles.

"He had only been up here seven or eight days," Castleberry said. "But when he was here, he acted like a regular guy. He worked the camps for us. He did what all the other guys in the Cape Cod league do. I guess he was tired of hanging around the house and wanted to come here and play."

Greer began his time on Cape Cod as a player, suiting up for the Chatham A's from 1965-67. Greer, elected to the Cape Cod Baseball League Hall of Fame in 2002, hit .349 in his first season and bounced back with a .368 average in 1966. Greer's Cape season in 1967, when he was a teammate of Thurman Munson, was cut short as he was named captain of Team USA for the Pan-Am Games.

"If you look at the league when I was playing, the coaches there were unbelievable," said Greer. "You had guys like Lou Lamoriello, Dave Gavitt, Bill Livesey, Red Wilson, Tony Williams, Tommy Yankus and (Joe) Skip Lewis. How can you get better coaches in the league? These guys were the top people in their profession."

Greer was the field manager of the Kettleers from 1979-1987. He was the third of three consecutive Cotuit coaches who successfully managed the franchise for exactly nine seasons.

"It's amazing, three guys in twenty-seven years," Greer said. "To

follow Jim Hubbard and Jack McCarthy—wonderful Cape Cod
league managers—was special. It set the bar for my goals. If I didn't
do my job well, I felt I would've let Jim and Jack down, along with
the town."

McCarthy guided the Cotuit club to four straight championships
from 1972-1975. McCarthy's streak ties a modern-day Cape record
for most consecutive championships by a manager with Livesey,
who did it for Falmouth from 1968-1971. In fact, from 1968 to 1977
McCarthy and Livesey were the only two managers to claim Cape
Cod Baseball League titles. After McCarthy's run, Livesey won the
1976 championship as a manager of the Wareham club before the
Cotuit squad won again the following season.

Hubbard began his time in Cotuit as a player in 1959 and sixty
before taking over as manager in 1961.

"At that time, I still played while I managed," said Hubbard.
"Then Major League Baseball got involved in 1965 and managers
weren't allowed to play."

Hubbard managed the 1964 Cotuit team which won twenty-one
consecutive games and could be considered one of the best teams in
Cape Cod league history.

"That 1964 Cotuit team was the best ballclub, in my opinion,"
said longtime CCBL umpire Curly Clement, who called balls and
strikes on Cape Cod for thirty-four seasons.

Greer was a player on the 1966 Chatham team, which featured
future Texas Ranger GM Tom Grieve. That squad could also be right
up there as one of the all-time greats after stringing together twenty-
three straight wins.

Even in the midst of his widely successful college coaching
career, Greer still reflects on his time on the Cape and remembers
nothing but positives.

"I look back and the one thing that stands out is the total Cape
experience and the addictive atmosphere you acquire when you're
there," he said.

"I always tell people that when I played in the league for
Chatham, I played for Joe Lewis, and I thought I was special playing
there. I was treated well and enjoyed my time there very much. When

I went to Cotuit, it was almost like being royalty. It was more than special. The sense of pride they have over there is unbelievable. They treat you very well there."

Those same sentiments are also expressed by the Kettleers' new field manager in 2004.

Mike Roberts, who had managed the Wareham Gatemen in 1984 and again in 2000, happily returned to the Cape Cod league for the '04 season.

Prior to being hired by the Cotuit club, Roberts wasn't shy about the fact he regretted leaving the CCBL after his second stint in Wareham, and he made it perfectly clear he desperately wanted one more chance at managing in the nation's premier amateur summer baseball league.

"The one thing I'm going to regret the rest of my life was resigning after the 2000 season," Roberts said before getting the call from the Kettleers. "I took an athletic director's job and it didn't work out for me and it's very disturbing to me. I'm working on a few important things in my life. I'm working on my doctorate right now, but if I could pick one thing to do every year for the rest of my life, it would be coaching in the Cape Cod Baseball League. I would drop my doctorate to coach up there again. I'd go as an assistant. It was that good of an experience for me.

"You really have to go to New England and experience the love of baseball for yourself. It's amazing the way the families open their arms to young men they've never met before. That's very rare, especially in these days."

In the fall of 2003, Roberts got a call from his new club and his wish to return to the Cape had been granted.

"I told John Wylde (general manager of the Wareham Gatemen) that if a position opened to please call me," Roberts said after the hiring. "He did that. He was nice enough to do that and he was just so incredibly helpful to me. I went and met the people in Cotuit and they were great. It was a wonderful meeting."

Roberts, whose son Brian is the starting second baseman for the Baltimore Orioles, also comes with a strong baseball resume as he had been the head coach at the University of North Carolina from 1976-1998.

"We were looking for someone who would promote a running game," said Cotuit GM Bruce Murphy. "He is one to do that and he was available. He's a great guy. We got a chance to spend some time with him and he's a hard worker with a lot of experience. We're very excited."

You'd be hard pressed to find a Cape Cod league coach who was able to get more out of his players than Don Reed.

Not only did Reed bring out the highest level of talent of those players, he turned them into winners as evidenced by his 334 career victories—a Cape Cod league record. Reed owns three more wins than Ed Lyons, who managed in the Cape from 1970-1982 and came back for stints in 1984 and 1989.

Reed also ranks third with a .606 winning percentage behind Lewis (.690 from 1965-1969) and Joe Arnold (.629 from 1980-1983).

"Don Reed is an old-school type of guy," said Eric Wedge, the Cleveland Indians manager who played for Reed in 1988 as a member of the Yarmouth-Dennis Red Sox. "There was a certain way he wanted things done and you had to abide by that, but we hit it off real well. He allowed me to go out and get the most out of that league. I was able to talk to him freely. He'd also listen. I wasn't afraid of confrontation and if I felt strongly about something, I'd say something to him."

"My observation about Don Reed is that the term old-school is a pretty good description," said John Wylde, the president/GM of the Wareham Gatemen, for whom Reed coached from 1991-1999. "He expected the kids to give their all. He was tough but that was his way to light that spark.

"I don't know anyone who took more pleasure in his players' future success. It was never, 'hey, I coached that guy in the Cape Cod league," but it was sheer, almost parental, delight. He had sheer joy for their achievement and it had nothing whatsoever to do with his ego."

Reed's passion for baseball can be summed up in one little incident in which he was playing ball back in Illinois with his sons

Jeff, who was a major-league catcher for 17 seasons, and Curt, who made it to the Triple-A level.

"Don was out on the field with his sons Jeff and Curt and a tornado or severe thunderstorm, I can't remember which it was, appeared," said Wylde. "One of his sons said, 'dad, watch out, look over the left-field fence,' and Don's response was, 'Oh, I see it, but we still have some more time.'"

On the Cape, Reed made sure his teams were fundamentally sound—even to the point where he would be bunting runners over in the early innings on some occasions.

That philosophy wasn't always well received by his players.

"I was only there about twenty games because I got into a conflict with Coach Reed," said Mikel Moreno, who played in Wareham in 1996. "Me and Dan McKinley came from Arizona State. Danny was a very good hitter and wound up being a first-round pick. One game, Coach Reed made him bunt in the second inning of a game. I couldn't believe it. Let him swing away. I thought that was horseshit. We had a difference of opinion and I ended up leaving. This was summer baseball and I didn't agree with the philosophy of taking it that seriously. I couldn't imagine doing that for another month. I might've been too immature at that time, but I have no regrets leaving."

Moreno, who was a teammate of Lance Berkman during his short stay, says the Houston Astros outfielder also would get on his coach.

"Lance had a big, smart mouth," Moreno said. "He had no fear saying things to the coach. He'd be in the back of the bus after a game and he'd say something like, 'great job bunting in the second inning, coach.' He'd say it in jest to rib him a little bit, but he was saying all the things I wanted to say."

Reed, however, had the backing of Berkman and his GM.

"I didn't start out great when I was there," Berkman said. "I think I was like two for my first fifteen or twenty, and Don Reed encouraged me to come to the park early. He and I worked every day. He was always working with me and he helped hone my swing. I have to give him a lot of credit."

"I'm not sure how much credit I can take," Reed said. "He's the one who showed up early. I could suggest it, but he came through by doing it. The big thing with Lance was that his mechanics were good. We just wanted him to get his foot down earlier and have him get a longer look at the ball. He came early every day and we worked on it."

"A lot of these kids are big fish in small ponds when they're at school," said Wylde. "On the Cape, they're normal-sized fish in normal-sized ponds. A lot of these guys, when they make it to the next level, are going to be called upon to bunt. If they're going to succeed playing wooden-bat baseball, they're going to have to learn to do these things.

"Don wanted to win. There's no ifs, ands or buts about that. He thought if the kids were winning, it would also make for a much happier summer."

Don Reed with CCBL Vice-President Don Tully
1999
Photo by Jeff Tamagini

Don Reed, right, is shown with former CCBL vice president, Don Tullie, celebrating Reed's 332 career victories.

Something often heard while talking to major league players who have experienced playing on the Cape is that they wouldn't be where they are if not for the Cape Cod Baseball League. For Ace Adams, that statement couldn't be any truer.

Adams, who was an assistant coach in the CCBL in the '80s and the field manager in Falmouth in the early '90s, had ties to Cape Cod long before putting on a uniform.

"My mother and father met at a Cape league game," said Adams, who also played for Orleans in 1972 and for Falmouth in 1973 and '74. "My father was a pitcher for Bourne in 1938. He picked her up at a game. I'm one of those guys who can truly say if it wasn't for the Cape league, I wouldn't be here."

Adams, now a pitching coach in the Boston Red Sox farm system, recalls his days as a player in 1972 when he was a teammate—albeit for just one day—of another major-league pitching coach.

"Joe Kerrigan was my teammate for a day," Adams said. "Joe came from Temple and he was one of the weirdest looking guys I've ever seen. He was like six-foot-three or six-foot-four and something like one hundred and ten pounds. He had curly hair, pimples. He looked like freakin' Bozo. He worked out for one day and then quit. I think we made him quit. The kids just made fun of him and he bolted."

In 1974, Adams got a taste of professional ball, signing with the Pittsburgh Pirates as a pitcher.

"I signed with Pirates in '74 for 500 bucks," he said. "I gave up a full ride at Michigan to sign. I went to Bradenton in '74 for one week and we played an exhibition game against the Cubs and I struck out seven of nine hitters. They released me the next day. They said I didn't throw hard enough. Then I started drinking heavily."

Adams began his Cape coaching career as an assistant in Falmouth in 1979 before taking other assistant positions in Chatham ('84, '87) and Cotuit ('88-'89). In 1985 and 1986, Adams worked for the Red Sox as a traveling batting practice pitcher. He got his first Cape managing job in 1992 with Falmouth.

"Ace is the best," said Mike Martin, a second baseman out of

Boston College, who played under Adams in Falmouth. "I don't know if I've ever played for a better manager. If you don't like the f-word, he's not your kind of guy. He's a guy who let you play.

"I came from Boston College and the Cape didn't give a lot of credibility to BC and for many colleges in New England for that matter. BC wasn't really considered a sexy school, and a lot of the players who go there and other New England schools were sort of blackballed. I was playing in the Bristol County League and Bob Curran, an assistant to Ace, called me and told me to come down in 1992. They needed someone for about nineteen to twenty games because someone on the team got caught shoplifting. I played for Ace in 1993, too, and playing in the Cape Cod league was an unbelievable experience—probably the best two summers I've had."

If there's one person who might surpass Reed in the all-time win department for a Cape Cod league field manager, it's John Schiffner.

Many people have referred to Schiffner as the "Cape Cod God," mainly because he has been affiliated with the CCBL for thirty-plus summers as a player, scout and has been the field manager of the Chatham Athletics since 1993.

"John Schiffner has more knowledge in his little finger than I have altogether," said Chatham president Peter Troy. "We are so fortunate to have him on our side."

Already, Schiffner has collected 243 victories as a field manager and he's still going strong.

"If there's anyone who's going to catch up to Don, it's John Schiffner," said Wylde. "He's got a great baseball mind and he's young enough where it looks like he'll be coaching in Chatham for quite some time."

Schiffner is so widely respected around the league that when *Summer Catch*—a far-fetched movie about the Cape Cod league released in 2001—actor Brian Dennehy played a character named John Schiffner, who was the field manager of the Chatham A's club.

Schiffner has many fond memories of his days spent on the Cape, and many of those date back to his playing days. Every once in a while, when he turns on his car radio and puts on that oldies station, he's sure to be reminded of Cape Cod League Baseball in the mid-70s.

"Whenever I hear a Frankie Valley song from the Greatest Hits album, I think of the '76 team," he said. "After a game, six, seven or eight of us would spend the evening at a cottage which had an old-fashioned record player with only one album—Frankie Valley's Greatest Hits. Whenever I hear "Walk Like a Man" I think back on those years. We were just a bunch of college guys having fun, drinking beer after the game. The drinking age was eighteen then, and we'd spend our money on beer instead of getting a new album."

Steve Ring began his field managerial career in the Cape Cod league in 1983 when he coached the Harwich Mariners to the league title. Ring's club, which defeated Greer's Cotuit squad in the best-of-five championship series 3-2, was led by future major leaguer Cory Snyder, who smacked a Cape-record twenty-two homers that season.

"Cory was a very, very, very integral part of us winning the title," said Ring. "But he wasn't there when we actually won it."

Toward the end of the season, Ring received a phone call from future 1984 Olympic head baseball coach Rod Dedeaux, who was trying to recruit Snyder for the Pan-American Games.

"He called me," Ring said. "I was at work. He wanted to know if I could get a hold of Cory Snyder so he could play for him. I was sitting at my desk, thinking 'hmmmm we're trying to make a run for the championship here. If I don't tell Cory about this phone call, he'll never know about it.'

"But I couldn't do that. I had to tell him. He clearly was our best hitter, but the right thing for me to do was inform him about the call."

Ring told Snyder about Dedeaux's call, and Snyder immediately turned to Ring for advice.

"He asked me what he should do," Ring said. "I told him there was only one place for him and that was to be out there representing our country."

"It was a tough decision," said Snyder, who was elected to the

Cape Cod Baseball Hall of Fame in 2003. "I was having a great time there and we were just about to play in the playoffs. It came down to a once-in-a-lifetime opportunity for me. I weighed my options and Steve told me when it came right down to it, it was best for me to go play in the Games.

"I went to play and most of that team went on to play on the Olympic team that following year."

One of Ring's strongest managerial qualities was clearly his ability to recruit. He traveled the country, taking in countless college baseball games to bring the most talented kids to Harwich.

"I would guess about seventy to seventy-five percent of the kids who played for me I personally saw," Ring said.

The coach also admitted he would go above and beyond to get that special player to come to the Cape.

Snyder was one of those players.

"I researched all my ballplayers thoroughly," said Ring. "Cory could've gone anywhere he wanted to play that summer so I had to find something special—something attractive—for him. Everyone has something about them that makes them tick or makes them happy. I knew Cory and his father were very tight so I told him we would bring his father along, too. I told him we would even find his father a job. Cory and his dad both showed up."

Ring also used a similar technique to try to get future Hall of Famer Rafael Palmeiro to play for the Mariners.

"Rafael Palmeiro was from Havana and I had a friend in the leather business," said Ring. "My friend would travel from Cuba to Boston, Cuba to Boston constantly. I was putting this all together in my head. I had him call Rafael's mother and father and told him to tell them if he came here, we'd find him a home where he'd have all the homemade Cuban food he wanted.

"The year before, he played in the Central Illinois league, and out of loyalty, he went back and played there again."

Ring even recalls a recruiting trip where two future major-leaguers had a run-in during a college game.

"UNLV was playing Florida State in a game and Todd

Stottlemyre was pitching for UNLV," Ring recalled. "The first three guys got hits off him and the next guy hit a grand slam. Paul Sorrento was the next batter and Stottlemyre fired a pitch that split Sorrento's helmet open. Wouldn't you know it, the next year these guys are playing for me and needless to say there was a little tension there. We had to take them aside and tell them to take it easy. Eventually, they soothed things out and everything was OK."

Ring coached in Harwich from 1983-1986, took a few years off and returned for a final season to coach the Mariners in 1992.

Even though it was only a six-year span where he went without managing, Ring noticed a huge difference in the players upon his return.

"In my opinion, the difference between the players in the early '80s and the '90s was like night and day," he said. "It was like the players in the '90s wanted to know what was in it for them. There were a lot of prima donnas. On paper, we had the best team, but we started out 4-16. Nobody came to play. We went 14-6 the rest of the way and missed the playoffs by two games."

The 1988 season was a memorable one for field manager Mike Kinnersley, who came to Harwich as an assistant coach in 1987 and thought he was going repeat that process in '88.

"We won the whole thing in 1987 under manager Billy Springman," Kinnersley recalled," and in 1988 I got to the Cape before the other Harwich coaches. I got a phone call from Billy, who said he couldn't make it there because he was interviewing for the Loyola Marymount job. So there we were with no manager and we had five roster spots to fill. We were supposed to have Bret Boone and Brett Barberie come that year, but they either signed or were swept away by Team USA. The GM and the president of Harwich got together and they promoted me to manager."

The loss of Boone and Barberie hurt the Mariners' chances of making the playoffs, as did an injury to pitcher Russ Springer, who would later go on to enjoy a fifteen-year career in the big leagues.

"He showed up with a tender arm," said Kinnersley. "He was a very good college pitcher. He and Ben McDonald were 1 and 2 at LSU. As a summer coach, I wasn't going to use him with a sore arm and send him back to school with his arm in a sling. He probably didn't pitch more than four innings for us and then he went back home.

"It was chaos to start because we were scrambling to fill some spots, but we ended up doing pretty well. We fell just short of making the playoffs, and in 1989 they brought me back to manage. Those seasons, 1987, 1988 and 1989 were by far and away my best days in baseball."

Kinnersley has a lot of fond memories of his time spent in Harwich, but the one that sticks out most involves the Mariners' late announcer Al Graeber.

"Al was one of the nicest men around," Kinnersley said. "Every single night, though, he would mispronounce my name. He would call me *Kinnserley*. I'm not kidding, every game he would do that. One night, someone actually went up to him and told him of the mistake. The next game he actually got it pronounced right but said, 'The Harwich Mariners are being managed by *Dave* Kinnersley.'"

Chapter 7

The Icons

"Arnie Allen really is a Cape Cod league legend. Everyone knows who he is. He's as important to the Cape Cod league as Frank Thomas, Jeff Bagwell and those guys."
–Matt Hyde, former Cape Cod league assistant coach

"If I had to use one word to describe Curly, it would be passionate. I remember his passion, his enthusiasm and his love for the kids. He just loved what he did. When you went to the park and saw him there, you were happy. When he walked onto the field, he had that extra bounce in his step, and he had that grin. He was an umpire junkie, and it would be nice if we were all able to love what we did as much as Curly did."
–Mike Coutts, former Cape Cod league field manager

For the Cape Cod Baseball League to be as successful as it has become, it takes a whole lot more than a quality performance on the baseball field. The reason the CCBL is ranked at the top of the amateur summer league list is because of those who donated their time and money to help ensure the CCBL maintains its high-quality status. These people have never played a game in the Cape Cod Baseball League, but are just as important as those who do.

It's people like former commissioner Fred Ebbett and former president Russ Ford, who teamed up to help bring wooden bats back for the 1985 season. That decision may have put the Cape Cod Baseball League over the top when being compared to the other summer leagues. Ford, president from 1978-1984, lobbied hard to get Ebbett to become commissioner, and the two helped bring the crack of the wood bats back to Cape baseball.

"I deeply respected Fred," said Ford of Ebbett, who passed away in May of 2003. "We worked hard to get the wooden bats accepted.

We were able to get the OK in 1984 and pro scouts were pleased and Major League Baseball was delighted."

Barbara Ellsworth has opened her home to Yarmouth-Dennis and Harwich ballplayers for more than twenty-five years, taking in total strangers as a host parent and cheering them on at each game.

It's people like these, and those listed below, who are the unsung heroes in making the Cape Cod Baseball League the best in its class.

CURLY

If there's ever a man who personifies the Cape Cod league, it's Curly Clement.

At the tender age of eighty-four, his memory remains as sharp as ever. Throw a name Curly's way and he'll quickly rattle off both the year and Cape Cod team for which the guy played.

He was called "Curly." He was called "The Candy Man." Judging by the fact he has umpired at every level imaginable, it's likely he's been called a lot worse.

Curly clearly remembers the good, the bad and the ugly from those umpiring days, which range from Little League all the way to the big leagues.

He recalls everything from the cherished friendships he created while working between the white lines to the heart attacks he suffered during the sixth inning in two different games. He is a story machine.

Robert "Curly" Clement was a permanent fixture in the Cape Cod Baseball League, umpiring the northeast amateur summer league for thirty-four years. Curly called his last game at the age of eighty-one, crouching behind the plate for nine grueling innings during the 2000 all-star game in Brewster.

"That was tough," Curly said. "Before the game I had both coaches, Mike Coutts (Cotuit) and John Schiffner (Chatham) come to the plate to go over the ground rules. I said to them, 'Listen carefully, I may cry. No, I know I'll cry. Mike, I umpired when you played in college. I umpired when you played in the Cape league, and now I'm umpiring when you're a manager. John, I umpired when you played in college. I umpired when you played in Harwich…' and then I started to cry. Mike leaned over to me and said, 'Curly, go ahead and cry. We'll cry, too.' They told me how much they appreciated what I did for them."

"If I had to use one word to describe Curly, it would be passionate," said Coutts. "I remember his passion, his enthusiasm and his love for the kids. He just loved what he did. When you went to the park and saw him there, you were happy. When he walked onto the field, he had that extra bounce in his step, and he had that grin. He was an umpire junkie, and it would be nice if we were all able to love what we did as much as Curly did."

"Passionate is the perfect word," Schiffner said. "I've known Curly since 1974 and he just loved baseball. He umpired at every level, and I think his favorite level was the Cape Cod league. He was quite the character."

"He had his own distinctive way of calling balls and strikes," said Arnold Mycock, the longtime GM of the Cotuit Kettleers. "He was very fair, the players loved him and he was a very good umpire."

"Curly was a hard-working umpire," said Dick Bresciani, the CCBL's former PR director who now works for the Boston Red Sox. "He loved the league and did a lot for it. He's a great guy who had a very tough job. Let's face it, as an umpire you're only right with fifty percent of the people."

"Everybody loved Curly," said Lenny Merullo, a long-time scout with deep Cape Cod league roots. "He loved the players and he loved to umpire. He once told me he wanted to be buried at home plate."

Players, coaches and fans grew to respect Curly, the lone man in blue inducted into the Cape Cod League Hall of Fame. He was enshrined in 2002, along with former players such as Nomar Garciaparra, Jason Varitek, Buck Showalter and Ron Darling. Former manager Bill Livesey, a Curly nemesis during their Cape Cod days, was also inducted that year.

"Bill Livesey hated umpires," Curly said. "Once you crossed that white line, you were his worst enemy. I remember umpiring a game when he was the coach at Brown University—they were playing Dartmouth—and Bill Livesey called time. He walked up to me and started yelling at me. I said, 'What the hell did I do?' That was on a Sunday.

"On Monday, I got a telegram that said I have been deleted from the umpire list. Bill Livesey had me taken off his games."

A few weeks later, they met again in the Cape Cod league.

"I told him he better never put his hands in my pocket again," Curly said. "He took money from me by taking me off the list. I think I threw him out twice in the Cape league that year.

"But let me say, we are very good friends now. He told me I was the best umpire the Cape Cod league ever had. And he was a great teacher. If I had a son who wanted to play baseball, I'd send him to Bill Livesey's school."

George Greer, also inducted into the CCBL Hall with Curly in 2002, played for Chatham in the mid-60s and later returned to coach in the Cape, managing Cotuit from 1979-1987. Today, Greer is a long way from Cape Cod as he has just completed a long tenure as the head baseball coach at Wake Forest University, yet his memories of Curly remain crystal clear.

"His passion for baseball stands out," he said. "If Curly saw some kids playing baseball on the side of the road, I think he would stop and watch them play. Curly would always find a way to get behind the plate. He'd officiate a game without being biased—the way it's supposed to be done. He genuinely and truly loved people who put on the uniform. He loved the game of baseball and loved being on the field. It's where he belongs."

Showalter, the Cape Cod league's batting champion in 1976 with a .434 average for the Hyannis Mets, respected Curly so much that when he became the manager for the Arizona Diamondbacks in 1998, he recommended Curly be hired as a scout.

Showalter and Curly have maintained a steady friendship, and Curly even took a trip to see the former D-Backs manager during spring training of '98.

"We went on vacation to Arizona and my daughter is a Colorado Rockies nut," he said. "So we went to see the Diamondbacks play the

Rockies. I went down toward the Diamondbacks dugout and the attendant said I couldn't go down any farther. I saw Buck Showalter on the field and just yelled, 'Buuuccckkk, Buuuucccckk.' He looked up and said, 'Hey, that's Curly. Let him down here.'"

While on the field, Curly also ran into a few other old friends in Walt Weiss, Joe Girardi and Marvin Freeman, all former Cape leaguers playing for the Rockies.

"I went to shake Walter Weiss' hand and he just hugged me," Curly said. "He said, 'I owe you an awful lot.'

"The friendships I have encountered with ballplayers from the Cape Cod league are out of this world."

Don Reed, a longtime coach in the Cape Cod league, who as an assistant at Chatham before becoming the manager at Yarmouth-Dennis and at Wareham, says Curly's induction into the Hall is well deserved.

"He was a great guy and a great umpire," said Reed, whose son Jeff spent seventeen seasons as a catcher in the majors. "He threw me out once. When my son played with the Rockies, we'd get together with Curly, whose daughter lives in Colorado. He was a good friend of mine. In fact, I've got a picture on my wall of Curly and me arguing a call."

"Curly's legendary," said Joe Walsh, the pitching coach for Wareham under Reed and currently the head baseball man at Harvard University. "There are a few people in Boston who are known by one name—Yaz, Nomar, Larry—and Curly's another one of them. He might not be headlined in the *Boston Globe* like those others, but everyone in baseball around here knows who Curly is."

It all started back in 1956 when Curly moved from Manchester, N.H. to Hyannis and decided to take up umpiring the following year.

"I worked five days a week for two years, umpiring Little League for nothing—no money," Curly said.

He then worked two games in the Cape Cod Baseball League in the 1961 and 1962 seasons before Adrienne, his wife of sixty-four years, suggested he attend umpiring school.

He took her advice, and the following year headed to West Palm

Beach, Fla., attending a camp run by Bill Howser, the brother of the late Kansas City Royals manager Dick Howser.

"After the camp, I was offered a job working Class A in the Dakotas for three hundred and fifty dollars a month," Curly recalled. "I said no and went back to the Cape."

His return home sparked a life-long umpiring career, which reached its pinnacle in 1979 when he got a crack at calling the shots in the big leagues.

"I was working at King's Department Store and I got a phone call," Curly said. "It was Haywood Sullivan saying the umps were going on strike and he wanted me to umpire the game that night at Fenway. I said, 'Haywood Sullivan? Bullshit' and I hung up the phone.

"Then I called my wife and asked if she heard anything about the umpires being on strike and she said she hadn't."

An hour later, the King's Department Store phone rang again.

"It was Haywood Sullivan again, and he said, 'Curly, we want you up here at four in Boston,'" Curly said. "I asked him who the hell promoted me. He told me his son (Marc, a former big-league catcher) had played when I was umpiring and a few scouts had recommended me."

Curly made his major-league debut that night, umpiring the Boston Red Sox-California Angels game, collecting one hundred and eight dollars for his efforts.

That game in 1979 was the only big-league game he took part in that year, but Curly was called upon again the following season to umpire the Fenway opener in 1980 against the Cleveland Indians.

"I wish I hadn't worked in '80," he said. "I was at second base and I called Carl Yastrzemski out. He just shook his head and said, 'nice call, son.' When I went back to work at King's, every day for about a month some woman would call me and chew my ass out about that call. And when she didn't call, she'd show up."

Curly, slapped with the nickname in 1934 by schoolmates because of his twisted hair (although Adrienne insists it was 'frizzy'), wasn't a big fan of his new identity.

"I hated it," he said. "But everyone was calling me Curly. Even my teachers didn't know my real name until they looked in the yearbook."

Curly also developed another nickname, The Candy Man, as a result of some unique umpiring antics in the Cape Cod league.

"I was behind the plate one game and the catcher comes over and starts talking to me," he said. "His cheek looked swollen and I asked him if he had a toothache. He said he didn't. He was just chewing tobacco."

Curly then drew a large circle behind home plate and warned the catcher.

"See this," he said, "this is my space. There better not be any tobacco in my space.

"He asked me what he should do and I said, 'I don't give a shit what you do, just keep it out of here.'"

The next inning the coach came running out of the dugout, asking the umpire what he had done to his catcher. With a puzzled look, Curly asked the coach what he was talking about. The coach replied, "He's sick, he just swallowed his tobacco."

Curly wasn't a big fan of chewing tobacco, so after the incident, he went out and bought fifty-five pounds of individual assorted candy, and randomly distributed them to players and coaches throughout their games.

"I did it so they could chew on something other than tobacco," Curly said. "The first guy I ever gave candy to?—Will Clark."

"I remember that," said Clark. "He offered me some candy and I said, 'are we supposed to be doing this?' He said, 'sure, it's OK. Take it.' The next time I saw him I said, 'boy, that candy was good. Got any more?' He reached in his pocket and handed me more and the catcher was looking at us wondering what the heck was going on."

The candy wasn't only used as a tobacco replacement; it also helped Curly avoid some bitter, in-game arguments.

"I was umpiring a game behind the plate in Wareham one night," Curly recalled, "and I heard some chirping. It was Mike Roberts, the Wareham coach, hiding behind a pole (Mike's son, Brian, was the bat boy for the Gatemen and is now the second baseman for the Baltimore Orioles). I told him to stop hollering at me. He kept yelling at me so I offered him some candy. He told me to shove the candy up my ass. I asked him if he was sure he didn't want any candy. After a few more words, Mike looked at me and said, 'Good job, Curly. Now I forgot what I wanted to argue about.'"

"The best umpires know how to get you distracted," said Roberts, who was the Wareham head coach in 1984 and again in the 2000 season. "He had a good knack for doing that.

"Curly and I had what I would call a few friendly disagreements, but he had great respect for all of us. He was one of the best. He had a great disposition. He was extremely honest and you could always tell he was doing his best. I remember the most fun I had in 2000 was watching him umpire the all-star game."

The Candy Man carried his antics outside the Cape Cod league, passing out the goods at the NCAA level.

"I played third base for the University of Maine," said Coutts, who coached the Cotuit Kettleers on the Cape from 1995-2002. "Curly would always come up to me and give me candy. Throughout the years it went from sugar candy to sugarless."

"When I umpired up at Providence College, I would always give Lou Merloni (Bourne-Cotuit, 1991-92) candy," Curly said. "He'd always come up to me and say, 'Curly, where's our candy?'

"Bruce Wheeler (longtime baseball coach at Division III University of Massachusetts at Dartmouth) refused to give me baseballs before a game unless I gave him candy."

When talking to Curly, the mention of the Cape Cod Baseball League brings a certain sparkle to his eyes, and the baseball stories seem to flow off his tongue.

There's the game in Chatham against Yarmouth-Dennis when Curly made more than a few Chatham players, coaches and fans unhappy.

"There were no lights," he said. "The score was tied 3-3 in the fifth inning and the Chatham coach comes out and says he wanted to change pitchers. I said OK.

"After the pitcher warmed up, the coach comes over to me and says he now wants to change catchers. I looked at him and asked him if he was sure he wanted to change catchers. He said yes. At that point, I know he's trying to delay the game because there are no lights, so I went right over to the scorer and said, 'The game is forfeited. Yarmouth wins, 9-0.'

"Then I started walking to my car and the Chatham coach follows me and tells me I can't do that. I looked at him, pointed to a shed ahead of us and said, 'See that shed? If you're still with me by the time we get to that shed, I'm going to kick the shit out of you.'

"I actually was glad he didn't take me up on that offer."

There's also the time when he was umpiring a Hyannis Mets game behind the plate and was whacked in the wrist by a foul ball, triggering immediate swelling. One of the coaches came over with an ice pack, prompting Curly to ask, "How the heck am I going to hold it on my wrist and call the game?"

The Mets' catcher turned around, offered Curly his wristband and the umpire put the pack on his wrist and held it together with the wristband.

"I said, 'Son, you're in the big leagues now,'" Curly recalls. "The catcher was Jason Varitek."

Curly also calls to mind the time when he was umpiring an NCAA tournament with three others at Clemson University. They would each take turns calling the games from behind plate and they had a five-dollar bet as to who would call the quickest game. In the fifth game of the tournament, Curly was behind the plate and was on pace to break Al Foreman's time, which was set in the opening contest.

"It was going along so fast," Curly said. "I was going to win. I was ready to collect my money, but game ended up going twelve innings. I lost that one."

The twelve-inning affair was nothing compared to the eighteen-inning stint he would later take part in during the New England Championships in Pawtucket, R.I.

"The game started at 9:15 and ended at 3:15 in the morning," said Curly. "The owner of the stadium, Ben Mondor, said, 'Curly, no more of those games. From now on, at twelve we're cutting the cable so the lights will go out."

There wasn't much that kept Curly from donning the umpiring gear. Not even the death of his dad.

It was in the early '70s when Curly's father passed away and Curly and his family drove up to New Hampshire on a Friday morning to attend the Mass.

"I got home later that night and at about 7:30 the phone rings," Curly said. "(Commissioner) Danny Silva called. He said, 'We're going to have to reschedule the game. We have no umps. I can't get an ump. I know what you're going through right now, but would you want to umpire?'

"I said, 'Danny, I'm on my way.'

"I remember the game. It was Chatham vs. Sandwich and I umpired the game—all alone. I even got booed for being late, but in the fifth inning they made an announcement letting the people know why I was late."

Some of the on-the-field acquaintances with Cape Cod league players have even reached the personal level for Curly.

"After one game I was at my car changing," he recalled, "and a guy comes over and said, 'Mr. Clement?'

"I said, 'Son, the game is over, my name is Curly.' He said he wanted some information, and I told him I'd try to help.

"He said, 'I go to Georgia. I'm a freshman. I know I can play in the big leagues, but I can't get drafted for a few more years.' I said, 'Son, I can't advise you on that. I'm not your father.'

"He told me he came from a broken home and didn't live with his father or his mother, so I said to him, 'I've seen you play and you are a prospect. Don't go to college. Go to a prep school or a junior college.'

"He ended up going to a junior college in Florida, and was drafted by the Houston Astros. His name was Glenn Davis."

Then there were the heart attacks.

"I was umpiring at BC, 1982. It was BC versus Maine," he said. "Bill Swift was playing for Maine then. I had the plate. In the sixth inning, I have a heart attack. I had to have angioplasty. In 1988, I was down in Florida, I had the plate. In the sixth inning, I have a heart attack. They had to ship me to Gainesville."

"I was at that game at Boston College when he had that heart attack," said long-time scout Bill Enos. "It was something like 100 degrees and he was wearing about three sweatshirts. They took him away in an ambulance and I rode up there to see him immediately."

While there were many ups and downs in his lengthy career, Curly admits there were many more positives than negatives. He remembers most of the players and has a short list of some of his top Cape Cod leaguers.

"To me, I thought Walt Weiss was one of the best shortstops I've seen," he said. "I remember when Nomar was playing, I told the Orleans coach he had a very good shortstop, but he couldn't hit worth shit.

"Jeff Bagwell was a good third baseman for Chatham, and Craig Biggio was a good catcher for Yarmouth, but a guy by the name of Matty Galanti, who played for Cotuit in 1964, was the best second baseman I saw."

Curly admits when he watches a game on television these days, he can't help but do a little critiquing of the umpires. He says, for the most part, they are doing a wonderful job.

"To me, I'd say ninety percent of the umpires in the majors are good," he said. "The strike zone, however, is a joke. What is it—from the belly button to the belt? In the book, it says it's from the knees to the armpit."

Curly took a lot of pride in his umpiring, making sure the calls were as accurate and fair as possible, but his main objective was teaching respect.

"For me, it was all about respect on the field," Curly said. "I would always say, 'Hello, Mr. Weiss or hello, Mr. Third Baseman.' I respected the players and wanted their respect. If you're feuding with them on the field, be professional and show respect. Don't swear at them. If you're wrong, admit it.

"Umpires are human and we're going to make mistakes. That's

why they have erasers on pencils. Danny Silva once told me if you work a nine-inning game and miss six to eight pitches, you're doing one hell of a job."

"Danny Silva took Curly under his wing," said Mycock. "He gave Curly his first umpiring uniform, and Curly took to him like a duck takes to water."

Silva was one of the many folks on Cape Cod who earned Curly's respect.

"I was very fortunate that in my thirty-four years with the Cape Cod league I had three of the best commissioners," Curly said. "Danny Silva—he taught me the ground rules. He taught me the fundamentals of umpiring. He was just a very nice man.

"Dick Sullivan—he was my guardian angel. It seemed like every time I'd get hit with a foul ball, I'd look up and there's Dick Sullivan. It was unbelievable.

"Fred Ebbett—I had Fred when he was coaching high school and coaching in the Cape Cod league. He was terrific. He was the nicest man you ever laid your eyes on."

Sullivan, who is the only one to be the commissioner and president of the Cape Cod Baseball League, recalls those days when he was there for Curly.

"Curly's the old war horse," Sullivan said. "One day he got hit with a foul ball and was out cold. He came to and told me to get him his mask. I told him there was no way he was going to continue and that he was going straight to the hospital. He was adamant that he was going to continue umpiring the game. Here I was on the field arguing with him during the game. Sure, enough he finished the game.

"He's special. I nominated him for the Hall of Fame. He cried for five minutes when I told him he was going in. He's an amazing person and all of his stories are priceless."

"I made a lot of friends in baseball," Curly said. "I'm very satisfied with what I accomplished. I supported my family, my four kids. I'm happy with what I was able to do. I just hope and pray I taught a lot of people how to behave on the field.

"When I worked in the Cape Cod league back in 1961, I made

eight bucks a game. Now they have three umpires per game and they get a hundred bucks each. That's the part that makes me a little sick."

ARNIE ALLEN

One of the most popular figures in the Cape Cod league never sported a glove, never scored a run and never argued a call. Well, maybe he argued a few calls, but Arnie Allen never was a coach, player or general manager in the CCBL.

"Arnie just completed his 46th season," said Falmouth general manager Chuck Sturtevant in August of 2003. "He's the equipment manager. He's in charge of the bat boys and making sure the game equipment is ready."

It would be difficult to find anyone more dedicated to the Cape Cod Baseball League, the Falmouth Commodores in particular, than Arnie Allen.

In today's world, Arnie would have been referred to as a special needs adult. He was a fifty-three-year-old man battling cancer, while his heroes were battling on the ballfield. The disease, however, didn't stop Arnie from passionately rooting for the men in maroon at Fuller Field in Falmouth.

Arnie's long-time dedication earned him a place in the Cape Cod League Hall of Fame as he was given the first Lifetime Achievement Award in 2002, the same year former players Nomar Garciaparra, Jason Varitek, Ron Darling and Buck Showalter were inducted.

"Everyone knows Arnie Allen," said Mike Martin a second baseman with the Commodores in the 1992 and '93 seasons. "This guy would ride his bike over the Bourne Bridge to get to a game."

"Arnie Allen was amazing," said Don Nestor an all-star relief pitcher for the Commodores in 1993. "When we got there, they were talking about this bat boy and he was like fifty years old. He was very dedicated. I remember when he missed his ride to an away game and ended up riding his bike there.

"One thing I really remember about him was that he had such an annoying voice, very scratchy. We had a pitcher out of Indiana who worked at Bradlees with a bunch of us and he could imitate Arnie's voice to a T. One day at work, this guy turns on the loudspeaker and makes this long announcement in Arnie's voice. We were crying because we laughed so hard. He was reprimanded for that—might've even gotten fired—but it was worth it."

"I would say Arnie's the most well-known figure in the Cape league," Sturtevant said. "He's very enthused, very focused. There are a lot of major-leaguers, whether they played for Falmouth or not, who know who he is."

Anaheim Angels players Darin Erstad and Adam Kennedy, both former Falmouth players, certainly know him.

"I remember one night the Angels were in Baltimore and I notified Darin that Arnie had cancer," Sturtevant recalled. "After they returned to Anaheim, Arnie was sent a box of two game-used bats from Adam and Darin, personalized to Arnie.

"At the (2002) World Series, in the seventh game, Darin and Adam saw Peter Gammons before the game and they knew Peter was going to be at the Cape Hall of Fame later in the year. The first thing they did was say please tell Arnie we're asking for him. That just tells you a lot about him."

On October 26, 2003, Arnie succumbed to the cancer, and days later he was buried in his Falmouth uniform, along with his Hall of Fame plaque and those precious autographed bats.

The Falmouth organization thought so much of Arnie, it has since named the baseball diamond at Guv Fuller Field after him.

"Arnie Allen, talk about passionate," said John Schiffner, the field manager of the Chatham A's who has been affiliated with the Cape Cod league for more than thirty years as a player, scout and manager. "I loved Arnie. He's priceless and such an inspiration.

"He loved the Falmouth Commodores. If you beat Falmouth, he'd be screaming at you when you walked by. He didn't like to lose. I'm sure everyone is saying all these wonderful things about Arnie, but I'm telling you, he could be a mean bastard when they lost. That just showed you the passion he had. He was a great guy."

"Arnie and I became very close in 1973," said Ace Adams, a

player for Falmouth in 1973 and '74, and later became the manager of the Commodores in the 1992 and '93 seasons. "He would clean out my car and I'd give him five bucks. Arnie couldn't read or write, but I can honestly say he had more common sense than anyone I've known. To me, he was a very special guy. He loved Falmouth, he even used to get thrown out of games."

Arnie did a lot more than just make sure the uniforms were clean and cheer for the Commodores. Sometimes, he took it upon himself to make sure the outfield grass was cut.

"He used to work for a landscaping company and on his way home he'd come down and cut the grass at the field by hand," Sturtevant said.

"Arnie Allen's a great story," said Cape Cod league president Judy Walden-Scarafile. "He was the cornerstone of the Falmouth team. He was a great part of that team and all the players and coaches loved him. He will be sorely missed."

"Arnie Allen really is a Cape Cod league legend," said Matt Hyde, an assistant coach in Chatham in 1995 and '96 and an assistant in Brewster in '98. "Everyone knows who he is. He's as important to the Cape Cod League as Frank Thomas, Jeff Bagwell and those guys."

DICK SULLIVAN

For Dick Sullivan, retiring from the Cape Cod Baseball League hasn't been easy.

Sullivan, who began his thirty-plus-year tenure in the league as commissioner in the early '70s, is the only person to hold the positions of commissioner and president of the league. Today, Sullivan continues to play a vital role in the league as deputy commissioner.

"I've had five retirements from the league," Sullivan joked. "I keep coming back. It's a labor of love."

"He's one person we're not letting go of," said league president Judy Walden-Scarafile. "We won't let him out of our sight. He's really been the glue to the league. He's won just about every award on the Cape."

One of the Cape Cod league's greatest accomplishments is bringing back the wooden bats in the summer of 1985. Former commissioner Fred Ebbett and former league president Russ Ford played a major role in taking the necessary steps to make it happen and get most of the credit, but it was Sullivan, who brought Ebbett aboard.

Sullivan also brought a lot more aboard.

He was responsible for getting Team USA to come to the Cape for an exhibition game with the Cape Cod League all-stars in 1984 and 2000. He brought in the Colorado Silver Bullets, a women's professional team, to Orleans for an exhibition game in 1996. These events drew huge Cape crowds and provided the league with some added exposure.

If there's a word to describe Sullivan, it's dedication. He is a prominent figure with the Cape Cod Baseball League, and his intense dedication extends well beyond the baseball fields.

In October of 2003, Sullivan was the recipient of the Elaine Whitelaw Award, for his dedication to the March of Dimes. The award honors the top March of Dimes volunteer in the United States.

"They kept it a secret from me," Sullivan said. "I had no idea I was getting an award. There were fifty-four nominees and I can't remember a thing I said during my acceptance speech. I was floored."

Sullivan's commitment to the March of Dimes has extended to the baseball fields of Cape Cod, but he's quick to deflect the credit to the volunteers and league administrators.

"We have the greatest group of people in the world working to help this league," he said. "We work year round. I've had so many fond memories of my time here, it's very hard to pick one. Just to see this league blossom the way it has is very special to me. All the money in the world can't buy that."

ARNOLD MYCOCK

There's something to be said about a man who's still living and has a prestigious award named for him. When a team captures the Cape Cod league championship, it earns the Arnold Mycock Trophy. That alone is enough to speak volumes of the effect this man has had on the CCBL.

Mycock became the general manager of the Cotuit Kettleers in the early 1950s and has been affiliated with the league ever since.

"I was the treasurer for nine years," Mycock said. "I've been on many committees. I made the schedule for many years up until 2003, but now a computer does it."

"He did that schedule by hand each year and that certainly can be very difficult," said league president Judy Walden-Scarafile. "He's not the GM anymore, but he's still very involved. He's on our board of directors. We'll never let go of him."

Under Mycock's guidance, the Kettleers proved to be a Cape Cod league dynasty, securing four straight league championships in the '60s ('61-'64), five more in the '70s, including four straight from '72-'75, and three others in the '80s. Not only did the Kettleers have winning in their blood, they had stability and a sense of pride, as evidenced by the fact the organization only had three different field managers in a twenty-seven-year span (each managed for nine seasons).

"Arnold is the best," said former Cotuit manager George Greer, who was the last of those nine-year managers behind Jim Hubbard and Jack McCarthy. "He really could be the nicest man in the world. In my opinion, if Arnold hadn't been involved in the league, it wouldn't be what it is today. He did so much in the '50s and '60s, helping transform it from town teams to college players. He was a trendsetter."

"The first true friend I made in the Cape league was Arnold Mycock, many years ago," said Sean Walsh, former GM of the Bourne Braves. "I had interviewed him for a story and was taken by his outright honesty. He was diplomatic, but genuinely kind. I haven't met anyone like him since, save one or two people, and am not sure there will ever be another like him. Many times we have sat at his little table in his little Cape Cod living room and went on for hours discussing the history and lore of the Cape league. He is one person I have never balked at helping—not that he needs it—and vow to help to the day he is no longer with us.

"I can see why the Cotuit organization enjoyed fifty years of success under his management. I'd walk through a wall for him, and I am sure that the young men who played for him would do the same. It's an ineffable quality he possesses, and it breeds a winning attitude."

"Arnold Mycock is the ultimate gentleman," said Bruce Murphy, the GM of the Kettleers. "He's such a throwback. He's an easy-going, knowledgeable person who I enjoy working with. He's been around the league for such a long time and he continues to attend every meeting. He still even cuts the field once a week. He remembers everyone—where they lived, what they did. It's amazing."

IVAN PARTRIDGE

Head out to a Cotuit home baseball game and there is a great chance you'll hear the same three words continuously rolling off the tongue of one of the Kettleers' biggest fans.

Take a gander over near the on-deck circle and you'll see the man who has made a living uttering the same expression time and time again. Those three words—"have a hit"—can be enough to drive Kettleer opponents crazy, yet serve as an inspiration to the hometown team.

"Have a hit, Joey, "... "Have a hit, Mark, "... "Have a hit Tony... "

Ivan Partridge has been uttering that same collection of words for more than forty years, cheering on former Kettleer greats such as Will Clark, Tim Salmon, Greg Vaughn, and John Franco.

"Oh yeah, I remember that guy," said Clark, who played for the Kettleers in 1983 and went on to spend fifteen seasons in the major leagues. "That's part of summer league—having fans like that. It's nice to know there are some fans out there who are into the game as much as you are."

"I've been coming to the Cotuit games for about forty-five years or so," said Partridge. "For thirty years, we'd come up here for summer vacation from New Jersey. It was a lengthy vacation so I'd go to the games for about a month or so. I retired in 1990 and moved up here and joined the Cotuit Athletic Association. I became active with the team."

Partridge's catch phrase began long before his time in Cotuit, but Kettleer fans, and those around the rest of the Cape, simply refer to him as the "Have a Hit Guy."

"Have a hit began when I was playing ball myself," he said. "It's just something I've always said to have a little fun. It's something that I can say without offending anyone. Sure, people around the league mock me a little bit, but it's really all in fun.

"Have a hit has grown, but I never intended for it to grow. I didn't start out to do anything special."

"Ivan Partridge coined that phrase and he'd stand near the dugout and drive some of the players crazy with it," said Arnold Mycock, the Kettleers former GM. "Someone gave him a shirt with 'have a hit' on it and then he had a few more made. He also goes around and passes the hat—in our case, the kettle—and tells corny jokes while doing it."

"He's a character," said league president Judy Walden-Scarafile. "He's such a sweet man. He's someone who sees the good in everything."

Not only does Partridge drive some of the players crazy, he even irks his wife a little bit, too, but that has nothing to do with his three-word slogan.

"I grew up, and still am, a Yankee fan as I'm from New Jersey," said Partridge. "My wife is from Washington and was a Senators fan, but now she's a Red Sox fan. Fortunately, we have two TVs. We spend time watching games in separate rooms."

JOHN WYLDE

John Wylde Announcing Game
1998
Photo by Jeff Tamagini

John Wylde is president/GM of Wareham Gatemen and has been a fixture in the announcers' booth at Spillane Field for many seasons.

Sitting in the stands at Wareham's Spillane Field, the voice on the loud speaker has a slow, deliberate distinction.

"Now batting, the first baseman, Mo Vaughn. First baseman, Vaughn."

While the words flow effortlessly off the tongue of Wareham president/GM John Wylde, who has been a part of the Gatemen franchise for twenty-plus years, his work isn't done when the hitter is announced.

Nestled in the scorer's booth behind the backstop, Wylde, pen in hand, keeps track of every pitch, acting as the team's official scorer and the "statistical guru" of the Cape Cod Baseball League.

"We call him the statistical guru," said Judy Walden-Scarafile, president of the Cape Cod League. "He's the one who came up with the research that there were 190 major league players in 2003 who had come through the Cape. He's responsible for that. Now, he's following everyone in the minors. He's always giving us updates on stats. He's a tremendous asset and he devotes so much of his time and expertise to the league."

Wylde got his start in the league back in November of 1983 after the Wareham club had refused to field a team for the playoffs in the '83 season due to a shortage of players.

Wylde jumped aboard, choosing to sponsor the team himself, and has played a vital role in the Gatemen franchise ever since, whether it's announcing, scoring, or simply being the one of the most gracious figures of the Cape Cod Baseball League.

"John Wylde is probably the most refined gentleman I've ever been around in my life," said Houston Astros outfielder Lance Berkman, who played for the Gatemen in 1996.

"You look up the word 'gentleman' in the dictionary and his picture is there. He is so down to earth and he makes you feel so comfortable. He is definitely one guy from the Cape I'll always remember."

For Wylde, baseball and statistics are a passion. When the Cape Cod Baseball League season ends, there is no offseason for Wylde. Although he leaves the recruiting to his field manager, he continues to work year round.

"From September to November, I'm usually working on stats, trying to find a way to make them more efficient," Wylde said.

Although he won't physically recruit his players, he keeps tabs on college players and will make recommendations to his field manager for the upcoming season. He does, however, limit himself to watching college ball primarily in the New England area.

"I usually don't go beyond that," Wylde said. "I get very queasy about planes."

John Wylde with Carlos Pene
1998
Photo by Jeff Tamagini

John Wylde is shown with former Gatemen player and current major-leaguer, Carlos Pena.

JUDY WALDEN-SCARAFILE

Judy Walden-Scarafile will tell you her claim to fame is being the first woman ever to be kicked out of Yankee Stadium press box. Everyone else is quick to point out she's known around the Cape Cod Baseball League for a heck of a lot more than that.

"It wasn't even for a Yankee game," said Walden-Scarafile of her heave-ho from the legendary field in the Bronx. "It was an all-star game between the Cape Cod league and the ACBL (Atlantic Coast Baseball League). They just told me to leave."

Walden-Scarafile has quickly climbed the proverbial Cape Cod Baseball League ladder, working her way from scoring CCBL games as a college student in June of 1970 to becoming the league's president, a position she's held for thirteen years.

"I was at UConn traveling with the team and I got to know Dick

Bresciani (the Cape Cod league's former PR man and currently the vice president/public relations and archives of the Boston Red Sox)," said Walden-Scarafile. "He gave me an opportunity to score Cape Cod league games at fifteen dollars per game and I jumped at the chance."

Walden-Scarafile maintained her scorer's position until Bresciani went to the Red Sox and at that point she assumed part of his PR position. From there, she quickly went on to become secretary, vice president and president.

One of her biggest supporters was former commissioner Dick Sullivan, who is the lone individual in the history of the Cape Cod Baseball League to hold the position of both commissioner and president. Sullivan respected Walden-Scarafile so much, he refused to take a position unless she was by his side.

"I stepped down as commissioner because there was a lot going on in my life so I took a breather," said Sullivan. "I was asked to come back as president, but I told them the only way I would do that would be if Judy was my vice president. I respectfully requested she'd be my vice president and I left no room for discussion. I'm no fool, she smarter than all of us.

"Judy had been the scorer, league secretary. She was very dedicated and I could see so much talent in her."

Walden-Scarafile, who was inducted into the league's Hall of Fame in 2003, has also helped the Cape Cod league with its financial necessities as she became the league's first director of corporate development has garnered more than thirty corporate sponsors.

"Judy does a wonderful job," said Sullivan. "She never had any children. The Cape Cod Baseball League is her baby."

Chapter 8

The Opponents

"I had never been interviewed on TV before. They gave me an earpiece and the guy was asking me questions and I could hear people in the booth talking and it totally confused me. I wasn't making any sense. I just said something like, 'growing up in the summer here and getting a chance to play against the Colorado Silver Bullets is just the gravy on the cake.' As soon as I said that, I wanted to get the hell out of there. That has to be one of the worst quotes ever. I wanted to say it was the icing on the cake or it was all gravy, but it came out wrong."

–Gus Quattlebaum, local Cape Cod leaguer who played against the Colorado Silver Bullets—a women's professional team—in 1996.

On Sunday July 21, 1996, baseball history was made during a Cape Cod league game, and the history maker, ironically, wasn't even involved with the CCBL.

The Colorado Silver Bullets, an all-women's professional baseball team in its third year of existence, came to Eldredge Park in Orleans to play game thirty-three of their fifty-two-game schedule that summer, taking on players from the Cape Cod league in front of 5,000-plus fans.

Kim Braatz, an outfielder out of the University of New Mexico in her third season with the Bullets, smacked a dramatic 320-foot home run off Hyannis pitcher Pete Princi (Wake Forest), becoming the first woman to hit an out-of-the-park home run in a professional game.

"Oh, what a feeling that was," said Braatz. "I was watching him warm up and he was very consistent with his fastball. I like low fastballs and I remember looking fastball when I was at the plate. I think it was the third pitch he threw and I wasn't thinking home run, I was just trying to make contact."

Braatz made enough contact to pull the ball over the left-field fence, sending the near-capacity crowd into a frenzy.

"I hardly ever pulled the ball," said Braatz. "I was notorious for hitting balls up the middle. I just happened to turn on this one and it made it over the fence."

"I had a good look at it," said Kathy Morton, who was the on-deck batter. "I don't think anyone expected it. I remember a lot of the guys were smiling when she hit it. It was almost kind of a no-way-did-she-just-hit-that kind of reaction. It was a pretty short fence, but I think it would've gone over any fence."

Another person with a clear view of the homer was third-base coach Bruce Crabbe.

"When she hit it, I wasn't thinking home run," said Crabbe, the hitting coach for the Oklahoma Redhawks—the Texas Rangers' Triple-A squad. "I was thinking let's go, let's go, just get over his head. Then when it cleared, I watched Kim throw up her hands and it was a nice moment. It was very exciting for the girls. Even when it was over, I didn't think about it too much because it didn't hit me that it was the first one ever hit."

"The crowd went crazy when she hit it," said Alyson Habetz, who pitched for the Bullets that day. "I think they were very surprised. It seemed like even the guys on the other team were excited, too—except maybe the pitcher."

Princi wasn't overly excited, but he certainly didn't let it get him down.

"When she hit it, I didn't let it affect me," said Princi, a local kid who grew up in Barnstable and pitched parts of three seasons in the Cape Cod league. "I actually clapped. I give her all the credit in the world. I definitely didn't serve that pitch up. She earned it. That was no pop-up. She hit that ball 320 feet or so. She was a very good hitter and I wasn't going to let that home run get under my skin."

Despite Braatz's shot, the Bullets, managed by former major league pitcher Phil Niekro, fell to the CCBL stars 4-1, and if it wasn't for some pleading by Braatz and a change of heart by Niekro, the magical moment never would have taken place.

"In 1994, I had a herniated disc and eventually had to have surgery," Braatz said. "Before coming to the Cape, we had just played a game on turf and that took its toll on my back. Before the game, Phil came up to me and said, 'Kim, you're not playing tonight.' I never, ever questioned what he did because he was like a father to me. But playing against the Cape Cod league players was so important to me because the competition was so great. It was a privilege to play against them, knowing they are the best of the college players and knowing many of them are going to sign and play professionally.

"I begged Phil. I told him I would sit out the next three games, but he told me he was concerned about my back. I know he was just trying to protect me, but I told him I was OK and just waited for the lineup to be posted. I wound up being the DH that night and, although I wanted to be out there playing, I was happy to be in the lineup."

Not only did Niekro get Braatz into the lineup, he also had to go the extra mile to get the home run ball back from a fan, who eventually negotiated quite a deal with the Colorado manager.

"Phil sent our clubbie to go out and get the ball for me," said Braatz, who still has possession of the souvenir. "The clubbie came back and said the guy wasn't going to give up the ball. Phil autographed a ball for the guy and that wasn't enough. Then he took off his Silver Bullets jacket and gave him that and the ball and was able to get it back for me.

"Playing for Phil was great. He was like a father to me—so much more than a coach. Sometimes he was a little overprotective of us. He would tell us to be very careful if we went out, that sort of thing. He was an incredible man and to share that moment with him was just great."

If just being a part of the game against the Cape Cod league was a miracle for Braatz, making the team in 1994 was even more impressive.

"I had just gotten back from playing softball in Italy in 1994," Braatz said. "I was very good friends with some of the baseball coaches at school and they told me about this new team forming and told me to get my butt out there and try out. I didn't know anything about the team. I was at the airport after visiting my mom and dad in Utah and saw a *Baseball Weekly* with a story about a women's professional baseball team being formed so I picked one up. I read up on it and read quotes from Phil Niekro and knew this was an opportunity for me. I never played baseball before. My dad signed me up for softball when I was about five or so, but I really enjoyed baseball."

"Kim was very aggressive at the plate," Crabbe said. "She had a real good base, very good mechanics. She had good bat speed. She was definitely one of our top hitters."

Habetz got her opportunity to play for the Bullets with the help of her famous baseball friend.

"I met Tommy Lasorda when I was about ten," said Habetz. "He came to Louisiana for a baseball clinic and was going to be the guest speaker. His plane was delayed, and I was standing there hoping he would sign my glove. When he came walking in, I asked him if he could sign it and people were saying he was running late and didn't have time to sign it. But he stopped in front of me and asked me my name, signed my glove, and gave me his business card.

"I wrote to him quite a few times and he always responded. Whenever he'd come to Louisiana, he'd invite me to come join him. As I grew older, we became friendlier and he even allowed me to take BP with the Dodgers. When I heard about the Silver Bullets, I called Tommy and he called 'Knucksie' and asked him if he had room for his adopted niece to try out. They invited me to spring training and it was a dream come true. Tommy Lasorda is my sports hero for sure."

During their travels, the Silver Bullets encountered their share of chauvinistic criticism. They heard how they weren't good enough to be playing against men. They heard how baseball is a man's game and they should stick to playing softball. Despite the negatives, they simply went out and tried to prove critics wrong with their performance on the field.

"They way I looked at it, it was a no-win situation for us," said Gus Quattlebaum, who played for the Cape leaguers in the history-making game. "If we do something well, we're supposed to do that. Our goal, at least my goal, was to go out there and not embarrass myself on TV.

"I remember I hit a double off the wall that should've been caught, and I popped up. I know the guy who hit before me struck out. It was an adjustment up there against them because they were throwing about 70."

"I remember the crowd was huge that day," said Brian August, an infielder for the Cape team, who played four seasons in the Yankees minor-league system. "I took them one hundred percent seriously. I just went out and played it like any other game. I got two hits and I know I popped up my first time. The pitcher was pretty slow and that was an adjustment we all had to make. The game was on TV. I know my mom was watching it live on TV and I didn't want to get embarrassed.

"You could tell they were good ballplayers. I think in the first three or four innings, they barely touched the ball, but you could tell by their swings that they were just missing. When she hit the home run it was 'oh, my goodness.' I looked at the pitcher and he had a smirk on his face."

"We played against a few teams where the guys didn't take us seriously," Braatz said. "Some of them were so out of shape, but they would bring in a pitcher like Ron Guidry to throw against us. We played against guys like Guidry, who could still bring it, Oil Can Boyd and Leon Durham. We had to be in tip-top shape and do everything perfectly just to compete with a lot of these teams, but we wanted to do this. We wanted to play against men, not in a women's league. Sometimes we'd come into a town and read articles in the paper saying we didn't deserve to be there. Some said we should be playing softball. I also heard a lot of stuff I wouldn't repeat. Some of that stuff motivated us and some we'd let it go in one ear and out the other. Guys would even be drinking before a game, but as soon as we would take BP, they'd get nervous, because we were a very fundamentally sound team."

Princi was one of those players who took notice during the pregame warm-ups.

"As a player, you take every game seriously," he said. "I watched them during batting practice and couldn't help but take them seriously. They were hitting a few home runs during BP."

"When we played against men, there were people who really put so much emphasis on male vs. female," said Braatz. "That was kind of degrading. When I'm out there on the field, I expect to be treated like anyone else. I don't expect you not to throw at me."

Braatz made that perfectly clear in 1997 when the Bullets played the Americus Travelers in Albany, Georgia. The Travelers played in an eighteen-and-under league, and according to Habetz, the young boys were humming from the get-go.

"They were like an American Legion team or something," Habetz said. "Ninety-nine percent of the teams we played against were very respectful, but from the beginning of this game the whole team was on the top step chirping. They were out of control. Every time one of our players went up to bat, their catcher would say 'you suck, you can't play.'

"I was pitching that game and I remember leaving the game with a 6-2 lead, and then our defense just fell apart. They took a 10-6 lead and then got on us even more.

"Kim got up in the ninth inning, we were all upset, they were still hollering, and she told the catcher to just play the game. The next pitch hits her in the head. She started walking slowly to first while looking at the pitcher, and he just laughed at her. Then she charged the mound. It lasted about three minutes or so. Punches were thrown. I wasn't able to get any in, but I got punched in the side of the face. We were on the SportsCenter highlights that night."

Unlike the Cape Cod league players, the Silver Bullets were using aluminum bats during that 1996 season, although they had used wood during their first two years. The move was made to level the playing field.

"At first, I was wondering why we were switching to aluminum," Braatz said. "We were a little discouraged initially because we thought we were regressing. But we realized we weren't as strong as the men and there were only like two of us who could go deep with wood. There's a huge difference playing with wood. You had to hit it on the sweet spot. I know in spring training, I broke at least five or six bats a day."

"When we were using wood, teams would bring their outfield in," Habetz said. "The move (to aluminum) was made to expand the offensive game."

Whether it was with wood or aluminum, Braatz's historic blast was a legitimate shot over the fence off Princi, who took his share of heat after surrendering the homer.

"I don't know how true it is but I heard when he went back to college to pitch, fans were chanting my name when he was on the mound," Braatz said. "I didn't see his reaction when I hit it because I was just so overwhelmed with what had happened.

"I did get a chance to meet him after the game. He shook my hand, and he was very considerate—not bitter—but I know he did get heckled for it."

"I don't remember them actually chanting her name, but we had a few Florida State guys on that Hyannis team, Randy Choate and Brooks Badeaux, and when we went back to school and played them, there were a lot of fans chanting 'Silver Bullets,'" Princi said. "I never let that bother me. In fact, stuff like that actually helped me get more focused.

"When she hit it, something clicked in my head and I was able to put everything in perspective. I thought it was good for baseball. She was simply a good hitter who hit a home run. I absolutely have no excuses. I've been through a lot worse things in my life than giving up that home run.

"Back then, I looked at it as a little bump in the road. It was something that built character. To be successful in this game, you have to have a strong mental game."

Princi wasn't the only Cape leaguer to get heckled that particular day. Quattlebaum joined him in the embarrassment department during a post-game television interview.

"I went to Davidson College, which I believe is still the smallest Division-1 school in the country," Quattlebaum said. "I had never been interviewed on TV before. They gave me an earpiece and the guy was asking me questions and I could hear people in the booth talking and it totally confused me. I wasn't making any sense. I just said something like, 'growing up in the summer here and getting a chance to play against the Colorado Silver Bullets is just the gravy on the cake.' As soon as I said that, I wanted to get the hell out of there. That has to be one of the worst quotes ever. I wanted to say it was the icing on the cake or it was all gravy, but it came out wrong. It's been eight years now, and I still haven't lived that one down."

Traveling became very tiresome to the Silver Bullets, but when they came to the Cape in 1996, they were welcomed with open arms, receiving the same treatment any Cape Cod league player would be given, including living with host families.

"It was the first time we'd experienced living with a host family," said Morton, an assistant softball coach at the University of Houston who was selected in the first round of National Pro Fastpitch League in 2003. "It was neat. We knew the guys stayed with host families and we enjoyed it. I think it's great how the people in the community there take in all these people."

"I stayed with a very nice family," Braatz said. "I enjoyed it so much. The people who ran the league did it right. We had a luncheon before the game, and everyone up there was very hospitable. The league is very professionally run. Just seeing how the Cape Cod league brought the entire community together was a great experience for me. It seemed to me that you weren't normal if you didn't eat, drink, and sleep baseball up there."

"I remember all the people there had a passion for baseball," said Habetz, an assistant coach at the University of Alabama. "One of the things I remember there was the ice cream. I think it was in Orleans or West Barnstable, but I remember a little ice cream place there that had the best ice cream I've ever had."

Former president and commissioner Dick Sullivan was responsible for bringing the Silver Bullets to the Cape in 1996, and his main objective was to show the people on the Cape and the Bullets a good time.

"I think we did that," Sullivan said. "We didn't put out our best club. In fact, we had tryouts for women who would play for the Cape team. We picked two of them and hit them one and two in the order."

Under the direction of Sullivan, who was the executive vice president of special events at the time, the Silver Bullets were just one of a handful of select teams to come to Massachusetts and take on a group from the Cape Cod league.

Mark McGwire (#41) flips the ball to Greg Swindell for an out during the game.

The 1984 Olympic Team, made up of former major-league stars such as Mark McGwire, Will Clark and Cory Snyder, came to Chatham and the teams put on quite a show for the 8,000 or so fans who squeezed into the park.

"I think by having Team USA here that year opened the eyes of many fans," said Sullivan. "It helped bring some publicity to the league."

Despite the wealth of talent on Team USA, the Cape Cod squad held its own.

"We lost 5-4," Sullivan said. "We were up 4-3 with two outs in the ninth. Oddibe McDowell was up with a 3-2 count and he hit a fastball over the plate for a home run. In the last of the ninth, we had the bases loaded."

"Playing there in 1984 was awesome," said Snyder, who had smacked a Cape Cod Baseball League record twenty-two home runs for the Harwich Mariners in 1983. "To get a chance to come back that summer to play in a place where I had just had success was great. There was a huge crowd that game—there were people everywhere. Besides the major-league parks we played in, the Cape crowd was probably the biggest we played in front of that year."

Sixteen years later, Team USA made a return trip to the Cape for the 2000 season in what was easily the biggest Cape Cod league event in history.

"That year, I remember saying I wanted to knock people's socks off with this event," said Sullivan.

Sullivan got his wish as 10,000 people crammed in to make up the largest crowd ever to see a Cape Cod game.

"We were busing people in," he said.

Sullivan organized a flyover with four jets, and had a team of skydivers come down onto the field to present baseballs to four people who were going to throw out the first pitch.

"The flyover came right on the last note of the national anthem," said Sullivan. "It was special. Gave me the shivers."

The skydivers also created a special, but not-so-smooth, moment.

"We wanted them to land on the field and present the baseballs to those who were going to throw out the first pitch," Sullivan said. "There were four of them. Three made it while the other one ended up in a tree. He eventually got himself out of the tree, jumped over a fence and presented the ball."

Like the 1984 game against Team USA, the 2000 version was also a barnburner.

The game actually ended in a 2-2 tie after 12 innings when the teams experienced a shortage of pitchers.

"That night was the greatest night of Cape Cod baseball I've been involved in," said Peter Troy, president of the Chatham A's.

The Cape Cod league treated Team USA like it does its own players, setting the players up with a host family for the few days they were here, and the Troy family happened to take in the ace of the Team USA staff.

"We were very fortunate to have Mark Prior stay with us for about three days," Troy said. "That summer, we hosted a player by the name of Tanner Erikson, who went to USC was a teammate of Mark. That's how we got Mark to stay with us.

"Mark Prior is such a quality individual—a total gentleman. He just oozed talent and he didn't have an ego. He was a lot of fun to be around and he had a quiet confidence about him."

He also showed those on the Cape he would be worthy of becoming the No. 1 draft pick of the Chicago Cubs (second overall selection) in the 2001 draft.

"Mark pitched the first six innings, I believe, and people were walking away from the plate just shaking their heads," Troy said.

That 2000 Team USA squad also featured future major-leaguers Bobby Crosby, Mark Teixeira and Xavier Nady.

"I think that game was a thrill for everyone involved," said Sullivan. "I think we did that one right."

In 1995, Sullivan helped bring the World Junior Championships to the Cape. Teams from all over the world, including Cuba, South Korea, Australia, and Canada, came to the Cape to play a round-robin tournament.

In Orleans, in front of nearly 6,000 fans, USA defeated Cuba in ten innings, but it certainly wasn't without controversy.

"Like we always have on the Cape, some fog rolled in, and the Cuban center fielder misjudged the ball in the final inning," said Sullivan. "They immediately said it was a conspiracy and that we made it happen. I actually had to go out there and explain fog to them."

Chapter 9

Hall of Fame

"It really was a great feeling getting inducted. It was a neat thing to come back to Cape Cod for those two days. The atmosphere on Cape Cod and the passion for baseball is just incredible. There's such a great baseball tradition there and it's like one big baseball family."
–Cory Snyder, Harwich '83

Located in Sandwich, Massachusetts, the Cape Cod Baseball League's Hall of Fame makes its home at beautiful Heritage Museums and Gardens. The league has housed its diamond heroes since 2000, when the first class of twelve inductees, consisting of players, coaches and administrators was introduced.

"I was flattered to be inducted into the Cape Cod Baseball League's Hall of Fame because there are so many great players who come through there," said Mike Flanagan, the vice president of operations for the Baltimore Orioles who was one of the dozen selected in the inaugural season.

Walk into the museum and you'll be overwhelmed with rare baseball memorabilia, donated by teams, players and fans. Some of the items include a Cotuit game-worn jersey from 1947 (its first year of existence), the baseball used in the Cape Cod league's first no-hit game, an autographed batting glove from Mo Vaughn (another first-year inductee) in his first season with the Wareham Gatemen and countless team-issued items. Each inductee has his own plaque, complete with picture and a personal quote.

Although the Cape Cod Baseball League has been in existence for more than a century, the Hall of Fame is still considered in its early stages. Like the league, however, the Hall of Fame continues to grow with rapid success.

"The Hall of Fame idea had been talked about for years and (former commissioner) Bob Stead took the idea and ran with it," said

Cape Cod Baseball League president Judy Walden-Scarafile. "He did a great job. A Hall of Fame committee then began working on the preliminary details. When Heritage Museums stepped up to the plate to develop a display, then things really began to roll."

Things have been rolling along so well that in three years, Heritage Museums has dedicated an entire building for the CCBL Hall.

"Heritage took the Cape Cod Baseball League Hall of Fame to the next level when they expanded the exhibit to include an entire building in May 2003," said Walden-Scarafile. "The exhibit is awesome and we are so indebted to Heritage Museums for what they have done for the league."

"In 2000, the Cape Cod league decided to have a Hall of Fame and they were seeking a home," said Sunnee Smith, Heritage's deputy director of museum programs and services. "Ironically, we were looking to change our military museum at the same time. It seemed to make sense."

That combination planted the seeds of a strong relationship, and the two have a contractual agreement through 2008.

"We don't know what the future holds," Spencer said. "We love having the Hall of Fame. It might stay where it is. We could expand the building. The league could decide to do something like create its own building. Who knows?"

Although Heritage Museums and Gardens is primarily focused on horticulture, American history and art, it certainly did its baseball homework to make the Hall of Fame the success it is.

"We actually went to Cooperstown to see how a Hall of Fame with national recognition does it," Spencer said. "We talked to people there and they were terrific. We try to do the best we can."

Also inducted with Flanagan and Vaughn in the inaugural season were other former big leaguers Thurman Munson and Jeff Reardon. Frank Thomas of the Chicago White Sox was also enshrined.

Terry Steinbach, Chuck Knoblauch, Robin Ventura and Darin Erstad were selected the following season.

In 2002, Nomar Garciaparra and Jason Varitek headlined those inducted, which also included Ron Darling and Buck Showalter.

Cory Snyder, Sean Casey, and Carlos Pena were inducted in 2003.

The Cape Cod Baseball League certainly does its part in making the induction ceremony a first-class event, holding the occasion at the Chatham Bars Inn, a 205-room luxury oceanfront resort. Many of those inducted, including those who have gone on to have success in the big leagues, take advantage of the opportunity to return to the Cape to relive their glory days as a Cape Cod Baseball League player.

"It really was a great feeling getting inducted," said Snyder who came in from Utah for the ceremony. "It was a neat thing to come back to Cape Cod for those two days. The atmosphere on Cape Cod and the passion for baseball is just incredible. There's such a great baseball tradition there and it's like one big baseball family."

2000 inductees:

Dick Bresciani, Bill Enos, Mike Flanagan, Ed Lyons, Thurman Munson, Len Merullo, Arnold Mycock, Jeff Reardon, Dan Silva, Frank Thomas, Mo Vaughn, Red Wilson

2001 inductees:

Cal Burlingame, Fred Ebbett, Darin Erstad, Chuck Knoblauch, Tony Plansky, Terry Steinbach, Robin Ventura

2002 inductees:

Curly Clement, Ron Darling, Russ Ford, Nomar Garciaparra, George Greer, George Karras, Bernie Kilroy, Bill Livesey, Paul Mitchell, Buck Showalter, Dick Sullivan, Jason Varitek

2003 inductees:

Ed Baird, Sean Casey, Joe Jabar, Noel Kinski, Jack McCarthy, Carlos Pena, Jim Perkins, Ron Perry, Jr., Cory Snyder, Pat Sorenti, Judy Walden-Scarafile

2004 inductees:

Roy Bruninghaus, Bob Butkus, John Caneira, Will Clark, Pat Hope, Eric Milton, Jim Norris, Don Reed, Dave Staton, Tello Tontini

THE RECORDS

CAPE COD LEAGUE MOST VALUABLE PLAYERS

	PLAYER	POS.	TEAM	COLLEGE	DRAFTED BY
2004	Daniel Carte	OF	Falmouth	Winthrop	
2003	J.C. Holt	OF	Brewster	LSU	Atlanta
2002	Pete Stonard	OF	Cotuit	Alabama	San Diego
2001	Matt Murton	OF	Wareham	Georgia Tech	Boston
2000	Mike Fontenot	2B	Wareham	LSU	Baltimore
1999	Lance Niekro	3B	Orleans	Florida Southern	San Francisco
1998	Bobby Kielty	OF	Brewster	Mississippi	Minnesota
1997	Carlos Pena	1B	Wareham	Northeastern	Texas
1996	Kevin Nicholson	SS	Wareham	Stetson	San Diego
1995	Josh Paul	OF	Cotuit	Vanderbilt	Chicago (AL)
1994	Darin Erstad	OF	Falmouth	Nebraska	California
1993	Jason Varitek	C	Hyannis	Georgia Tech	Seattle
1992	Rick Ellstrom	3B	Cotuit	University of Miami	San Diego
1991	Brent Killen	1B	Y-D	Florida	Detroit
1990	Mark Smith	OF	Wareham	USC	Baltimore
1989	Kurt Olson	1B	Y-D	Indiana	Philadelphia
1988	David Staton	1B	Brewster	Orange Coast CC	San Diego

1987	Mick Morandini	SS	Y-D	Indiana	Philadelphia
1986	Scott Hemond	OF/C	Harwich	South Florida	Oakland
1985	Greg Vaughn	OF	Cotuit	Sacramento CC	Milwaukee
1984	Joey Cora	2B	Chatham	Vanderbilt	San Diego
1983	Greg Lotzar	OF	Cotuit	Central Michigan	Boston
1982	Terry Steinbach	1B	Cotuit	Minnesota	Oakland
1981	John Morris	OF	Wareham	Seton Hall	Kansas City
1980	Ron Darling	OF/P	Cotuit	Yale	Texas
1979	Ronnie Perry	3B	Hyannis	Holy Cross	Chicago (AL)
1978	Bill Schroeder	C	Hyannis	Clemson	Milwaukee
1977	Steve Balboni	1B	Y-D	Eckerd	NY (AL)
1976	Nat Showalter	OF	Hyannis	Mississippi State	NY (AL)
1975	Paul O'Neill	3B	Cotuit	Boston College	San Diego
1974	Phil Welch	P	Wareham	Providence	Boston
1973	Steve Newell	OF	Wareham	UMass	Montreal
1972	Brad Linden	1B	Orleans	UConn	
1971	Joe Barkauskas	C	Wareham	Lafayette	NY (AL)
1970	Jim Prete	2B	Wareham	New Mexico Highlands	Washington
1969	Jim Norris	OF	Orleans	Maryland	Cleveland

1968	Dick Licini	1B	Bourne	Notre Dame	Boston
1967	Thurman Munson	C	Chatham	Kent State	NY (AL)
1966	Ed Drucker	1B	Harwich	Southern Conn.	
1965	Ron Bugbee	3B	Sagamore	UConn	
1964	Ken Huebner	OF/P	Cotuit	Florida Southern	Philadelphia

Cape Cod League Batting Champions

	PLAYER	POS.	TEAM	COLLEGE	AVG.	DRAFTED BY
2004	Ryan Patterson	OF	Brewster	LSU	.327	
2003	J.C. Holt	OF	Brewster	LSU	.388	Atlanta
2002	Pete Stonard	OF	Cotuit	Alabama	.348	San Diego
2001	Eric Reed	OF	Wareham	Texas A&M	.365	Florida
2000	Steve Stanley	OF	Brewster	Notre Dame	.329	Oakland
1999	Jaime Bubela	OF	Wareham	Baylor	.370	Seattle
1998	Bobby Kielty	OF	Brewster	Mississippi	.384	Minnesota
1997	Jason McConnell	2B	Y-D	Arkansas	.345	Minnesota
1996	Lance Berkman	OF	Wareham	Rice	.352	Houston
1995	Josh Paul	OF	Cotuit	Vanderbilt	.364	Chicago (AL)
1994	Jon Petke	OF	Y-D	Cal-Berkeley	.379	Cleveland
1993	Jason Varitek	C	Hyannis	Georgia Tech	.371	Seattle
1992	Lou Merloni	2B	Cotuit	Providence	.321	Boston
1991	Mike Hickey	IF	Wareham	Texas A&M	.366	Seattle
1990	Mark Smith	OF	Wareham	USC	.408	Baltimore
1989	Bob Rivell	IF	Bourne	Virginia	.358	San Diego
1988	Chuck Knoblauch	SS	Wareham	Texas A&M	.361	Minnesota
1987	Mickey Morandini	SS	Y-D	Indiana	.376	Philadelphia

187

1986	Scott Hemond	OF/C	Harwich	South Florida	.358	Oakland
1985	Tim McIntosh	C/DH	Chatham	Minnesota	.392	Milwaukee
1984	Jim McCollum	1B	Falmouth	Clemson	.413	California
1983	Greg Lotzar	OF	Cotuit	Central Michigan	.414	Boston
1982	Terry Steinbach	1B	Cotuit	Minnesota	.431	Oakland
1981	Sam Nattile	OF	Falmouth	Central Florida	.443	Boston
1980	Brick Smith	1B	Hyannis	Wake Forest	.391	Seattle
1979	Ross Jones	OF	Hyannis	University of Miami	.407	Los Angeles
1978	Randy LaVigne	OF	Cotuit	UConn	.370	Chicago (AL)
1977	Del Bender	OF	Cotuit	Mississippi State	.395	Boston
1976	Nat Showalter	OF	Hyannis	Mississippi State	.434	New York (AL)
1975	Paul O'Neill	3B	Cotuit	Boston College	.358	San Diego
1974	Pete Ross	OF	Yarmouth	Michigan	.357	
1973	Dave Bergman	1B	Chatham	Illinois State	.341	New York (AL)
1972	Ed Orrzzo	C	Falmouth	Stanford	.372	
1971	Ken Doria	OF	Chatham	Florida State	.346	
1970	Mike Eden	3B	Orleans	Brevard JC	.378	San Francisco
1969	Jim Norris	OF	Orleans	Maryland	.415	Cleveland
1968	Dick Licini	1B	Bourne	Notre Dame	.382	Boston
1967	Thurman Munson	C	Chatham	Kent State	.420	New York (AL)
1966	Tom Weir	C	Chatham	BYU	.420	Boston
1965	John Awdycki	OF	Orleans	UMass	.407	
1964	Harry Nelson	OF/P	Bourne	Wagner	.390	New York (AL)
1963	Ken Voges	OF	Chatham	Texas Lutheran	.505	Chicago (NL)

CAPE CRUSADERS

Outstanding Pitcher Award
B.F.C. Whitehouse Award

Year	Pitcher	Team	School	Record	ERA	Drafted by
2004	Matt Goyen	Brewster	Georgia College	5- 2	1.25	
2003	Eric Beattie	Bourne	Tampa	4-0	0.39	Detroit
2002	Brian Rogers	Orleans	Georgia Southern	4-0	0.40	Detroit
2001	Chris Leonard	Wareham	Miami University	6-0	0.98	Toronto
2000	Ben Crockett	Wareham	Harvard	5-1	2.95	Boston
2000	Dan Krines	Chatham	Fairfield	7-1	2.01	
1999	Pat Pinkman	Wareham	VA. Tech	7-2	1.34	
1999	Rik Currier	Chatham	USC	7-0	1.34	NY (AL)
1998	Phil Devey	Wareham	SW Louis.	5-3	1.88	Los Angeles
1998	Jeff Heaverlo	Cotuit	Washington	7-1	3.09	Seattle
1997	Brent Hoard	Harwich	Stanford	2-1	0.72	Minnesota
1996	Billy Coleman	Harwich	W. Mich.	6-3	1.77	Minnesota
1995	Eddie Yarnall	Harwich	LSU	5-1	1.85	NY (NL)
1995	Jason Ramsey	Chatham	UNC-Wilm.	5-1	1.14	

1994	Bob St. Pierre	Falmouth	Richmond	9-1	1.44	NY (AL)
1993	Andy Taulbee	Y-D	Clemson	7-2	1.08	St. Louis
1992	John Kelly	Cotuit	UConn	7-1	1.20	NY (AL)
1991	Bill Wissler	Bourne	Penn	6-4	1.96	Minnesota
1990	Bill Wissler	Bourne	Penn	8-2	1.56	Minnesota
1989	Mike Hostetler	Cotuit	Geo. Tech	6-2	1.62	Atlanta
1998	John Thoden	Wareham	UNC	9-1	2.43	Montreal
1987	Pat Hope	Hyannis	Okla. State	11-1	2.27	Minnesota
1986	Jack Armstrong	Wareham	Rider	8-2	3.02	Cincinnati
1985	John Howes	Orleans	Indiana St.	7-4	1.81	Montreal
1984	Bill Cunningham	Wareham	Ohio State	6-4	2.54	Montreal
1983	Dennis Livingston	Wareham	Okla. State	7-2	2.84	Los Angeles
1982	Scott Murray	Harwich	New Haven	7-1	2.17	NY (NL)
1981	Greg Myers	Harwich	Cornell	7-3	3.88	
1980	Joe Pursell	Cotuit	Tulane	7-1	2.93	Toronto
1979	Walt Terrell	Chatham	Morehead	9-4	2.20	Texas
1978	Chuck Dale	Orleans	Florida	7-1	2.59	Boston
1977	Karl Steffen	Wareham	Ithaca	7-0	2.73	NY (AL)
1976	Mickey O'Connor	Chatham	St. John's	9-0	1.07	Minnesota

1975	Jerry Hoffman	Wareham	St. Mary's	8-3	2.33	Minnesota
1974	Andy Muhlstock	Harwich	Penn	6-4	1.09	San Fran.
1973	John Caniera	Chatham	E. Conn	9-1	1.37	California
1972	John Caniera	Bourne	E. Conn	8-4	1.86	California
1971	Bob Majczan	Wareham	Villanova	9-2	1.56	NY (AL)
1970	Paul Mitchell	Falmouth	Old Dom.	8-1	1.47	Baltimore
1969	Paul Mitchell	Falmouth	Old Dom.	8-3	1.20	Baltimore
1968	Paul Corddry	Orleans	Maryland	9-2	1.76	Boston
1967	Joe Jabar	Chatham	Colby	7-0	1.23	Seattle
1966	Joe Jabar	Chatham	Colby	7-0	1.53	Seattle
1965	Noel Kinski	Sagamore	Providence	10-1	1.91	
1964	Bernie Kilroy	Cotuit	BC	8-0	1.44	

Statistics courtesy of the Cape Cod Baseball League.

What the pros had to say about playing in the Cape Cod Baseball League

It was my first wooden-bat experience and I remember in my first game I had a real good swing and hit a dribbler down the line and just said 'oh man, I've got to get used to swingin' this lumber.' I didn't play as well as I wanted to—I think I ended up hitting something like .205. I was very tired after a long season, so in the long run, I'd say (the CCBL) prepared me for what to expect when I got to the big leagues.
    –CASEY BLAKE (1993, Hyannis)

The year before I played in the Cape league, I played in the Alaska league. I loved playing in the Alaska League, but I wanted to go back east to see the other talent out there and I also wanted to show myself to another part of the country. I'd say the leagues were very comparable. There was a lot more traveling in Alaska as the cities are a lot farther apart. The talent was also comparable, but I would say the Cape Cod league might have had a little better talent because most of the players in Alaska were from the West Coast and the Cape Cod league had people from all over.
    –CORY SNYDER (1983, Harwich)

The summer I played in the Cape is as vivid as any of the summers I spent in the majors.
    –MIKE FLANAGAN (1972, Falmouth)

Probably the worst part about having a pro career was not being able to go back to the Cape in the summertime.
    –WILL CLARK (1983, Cotuit)

I absolutely loved my time on the Cape. Think about it, you're 19-20, getting semi-paid—I mean you're working a job, but you wouldn't have that job if you weren't playing ball. You have no debts, you're playing six days a week and you're getting recognized. How bad can that be?
    –TERRY STEINBACH (1982, Cotuit)

It's a neat deal playing there—the wood bats, the level of competition and you get to experience playing every day. They do a very good job of recruiting. The teams up there keep their finger on the college pulse. The pitchers all have good stuff and everyone in the Cape deserves to be there. It's definitely a big benefit to play up there.

–LANCE BERKMAN (1996, Wareham)

I'm prejudiced, but prestige-wise I'd say it's the best amateur summer league. The whole experience was great. Ninety-eight percent of the kids playing in the Cape league have the ambition to go on professionally and that, to me, made playing more interesting. I got a real good taste of what it was like to play at the next level.

–BILL ALMON (1972, Falmouth)

I hadn't used a wooden bat since maybe Little League. I think everyone probably had trouble adjusting the first week. You start to get used to it when you're around it all the time and then you learn to make the adjustments. The fun part of the league was using those wooden bats and playing against a lot of very good players.

–ROBIN VENTURA (1987, Hyannis)

I wanted to play in a wooden bat league and the Cape was the best for that. If you can hold your own in that league, you can make it. You're playing the best of the best and you get a true feeling for how good you are. It's a great barometer.

–ERIC WEDGE (1988, Yarmouth-Dennis)

I sort of felt out of place at first, because I was with guys who I was reading about in Baseball America *and everyone there showed up in their team garb and I just had on a t-shirt and some shorts. I didn't feel intimidated, though. Once I got over that little hurdle, I felt like I belonged there and I realized baseball was still baseball.*

–CHARLIE NAGY (1987, Harwich)

CPSIA information can be obtained at www.ICGtesting.com
225581LV00004B/21/P